NOTES AND REVIEWS

NOTES AND REVIEWS

By

Henry James

With a Preface by PIERRE DE CHAIGNON LA ROSE

A Series of Twenty-five Papers Hitherto Unpublished in Book Form

---

Essay Index Reprint Series

Originally published by:

DUNSTER HOUSE

BOOKS FOR LIBRARIES PRESS, INC.

FREEPORT, NEW YORK

First Published 1921
Reprinted 1968

LIBRARY OF CONGRESS CATALOG CARD NUMBER:
68-22100

Preface

THE youthful Henry James, a few months beyond the age of twenty-one, began his literary career as critic, in *The North American Review* of October, 1864, with an unsigned review of Nassau W. Senior's "Essays on Fiction." In the present volume the editor has collected all of James's printed writings during the first three calendar years of his apprenticeship (1864, 1865, and 1866), with the exception of six papers which have already appeared in "book form." Of these six, two are stories: "A Landscape Painter" (*The Atlantic Monthly*, February, 1866) and "A Day of Days" (*The Galaxy*, June 15, 1866). Both were reprinted by Henry James himself in his collection of tales called "Stories Revived" (1865). The other four are unsigned book-reviews and may be found in Mr. Le Roy Phillips's volume of "Views and Reviews" (1908). These are "Matthew Arnold's Essays" (from *The North American Review*, July, 1865), "Mr. Walt Whitman" (from *The Nation*, November 16, 1865), "The Limitations of Dickens" (from *The Nation*, December 21, 1865), and "The Novels of George Eliot" (from *The Atlantic Monthly*, October, 1866).

The re-publication of the twenty-five papers

v

PREFACE

contained in this volume, all unsigned book-reviews from either *The North American Review* or *The Nation*, is an attempt, not at predatory "book-making" in the manner of the egregious Mr. Wise or Mr. Shorter for the sake of unrestrained "collectors," but at presenting to the many lovers of Henry James, in a worthy form, a series of his writings hitherto comparatively inaccessible which may fairly be considered to constitute his literary journal — his reading from day to day and his passing but considered critical reactions thereon.

To reprint all the forgotten and unsigned journalistic scraps of an eminent author, fleeting papers which he himself refrained from reordering and reissuing, is often to do his memory a cruel disservice. For many of the most eminent men of letters have been obliged, especially in youth, to stoop to "pot-boiling," and many under the shelter of anonymity have lapsed into the common frailty of haste and slovenliness. The average "gentleman's library" is freighted with vast, polyteuchal, "definitive" editions of popular great authors which, to a literary taste as sensitive, let us say, as James's, would seem very largely impressive monuments to national deforestation rather than to a discriminating national literacy. But in the case of Henry James, fortunately or otherwise, we shall, I feel, be spared a completely "definitive" edition. A few devout Jacobites, the editor included, will regret this; but the reason is

not far to seek. James, despite his present post-
humous eminence, was never a "popular" author;
and even the most devout Jacobite must admit,
albeit with serene tranquillity, that he was not a
"great" one. This is not quite the place to enter
upon a discussion of fundamentals. I may be
permitted to waive the point and aver merely, to
the common agreement, that his work was endowed with a distinction and a personal charm
which, to ears attuned to his peculiar appeal, will
always be unrivalled. He was decidedly what he
himself would have called a "special case." Even
his youthful journalistic work will at once strike
his accustomed readers as redolent of his personal
"note." It was not "pot-boiling," as he was
never quite under the economic necessity which
resorts to that; and this being so, it could not be,
with his temperament, either hasty or slovenly,
however impenetrably anonymous. One may ac-
quit oneself, therefore, of any disservice to his
fine memory in collecting his early papers to give
them out to his friends and lovers. One may
even go to the lengths he prescribed in the case
of Geoffrey Aspern, if in so doing one, as it were,
draws from an old cabinet, in this instance un-
locked, a forgotten daguerreotype of the '60's, a
portrait for which he knowingly sat and himself
autographed — eager, fresh, and charming.

But before analysing the revealing young portrait which these papers present, it will be well to
consider for a moment the general literary task

PREFACE

with which they concern themselves — that of "book-reviewing." Nowadays, unfortunately, in America at least, one must discriminate between the art of literary criticism and the trade of book-reviewing. Originally one and the same thing, to-day, thanks to a commercialized press and a generation of publishers who regard their operations chiefly as a species of speculative manufacturing, in the United States what was once the art of reviewing has sunk to a level of degradation where it either contents itself with the dullest of pedestrian comment or is indistinguishable from the publisher's unenlightened paid advertisement. In general, it is so abysmally and notoriously beneath contempt that it is scarcely worth while to mention the fact. It is, however, worth while, I think, to point out that half a century ago the case was quite different, that reviewing was among us by no means contemptible, and that not the least promising among our anonymous critics was a youth of twenty-one who quickly assumed an easy and distinguished posture among his elders in *The North American Review*. In the beginning, Henry James's critical performances were not, of course, "first-rate," — his youth, if nothing else, would militate against that. I am willing, reluctantly, to admit that, to the end, he was not a "great" critic: his steady preoccupation with problems of technique rendered that ultimate philosophical eminence unattainable (a constant, tragic paradox in all art).

PREFACE

But even at the beginning his work was informed with distinction, distinction of thought and of expression. If one feels that he is occasionally ineffectual, because he was groping for a literary "form" which his youth had not yet achieved, one is never unaware of the charm with which his groping naturally invests itself. And so, if it served no other purpose, this collection of reviews by a youthful fellow-craftsman, now among the august dead, might, if studied seriously by reviewers of to-day in America, tend to revive a well-nigh extinct art; for these papers, whatever their faults, are the expression of an alert spirit, a discriminating intelligence, ardently devoting itself with rare singleness of purpose to a service the rewarding beauty of which it never doubts. Yet, after all, the chief function which this collection will perform, and one most welcomed by James's own faithful circle of readers, is that of self-portraiture.

By a singular felicity of chance, the series opens with a discussion of the art of fiction itself, the art which James was later to cultivate with such assiduity and peculiar success. His ingenuous statement of the "fictitious writer's" problem (he does make this single engaging slip!) is a bit of unconscious prophecy, a programme which he was himself to follow undeviatingly: what he wrote at twenty-one through divination, he might well have repeated at seventy in the light of experience. "The friends of a prolific novelist," he sug-

PREFACE

gests, "must be frequently tempted to wonder at the great man's fertility of invention and to deprecate its moral effects . . . to which the prolific novelist will probably reply. . . . 'Just as the habitually busy man is the best novel-reader, so he is the best novel-writer; so the best novelist is the busiest man. It is, as you say, because I "grind out" my men and women that I endure them. It is because I create them by the sweat of my brow that I venture to look them in the face. My *work* is my salvation. If this great army of puppets came forth at my simple bidding, then indeed I should die of their senseless clamor. But as the matter stands, they are my very good friends. The pains of labor regulate and consecrate my progeny. . . . If the novelist endowed with the greatest "facility" ever known wrote with a tenth part of the ease attributed to him, then again his self-sufficiency might be a seventh wonder. But he only half suffices to himself, and it is the constant endeavor to supply the missing half, to make both ends meet, that reconciles him to his occupation.'" "The Missing Half," by Henry James: here, I propound, is a general title in his own arresting vein for the long series of his own reconciliatory "Comédie Humaine."

Among the list of writers whom James discusses in this volume are an exceptional number of names which have weathered the last half-century, some of the first importance, some of secondary but still enduring worth; only a few will be unknown to his younger readers. One will be amused, and if a confirmed Jacobite not at all surprised, to see how time has in general confirmed the early judgments of the youthful critic. And readers who themselves have ever ventured into "reviewing" will at once seek out with curiosity the grounds and terms of the critic's likes and dislikes.

The grounds of some few of James's dislikes are certainly constitutional. I, for one, in view of the future "Turn of the Screw" and "What Maisie Knew," have been perhaps unreasonably diverted by this little passage: "The heroine of 'Moods' is a fitful, wayward, and withal most amiable young person, named Sylvia. We regret to say that Miss Alcott takes her up in her childhood. We are utterly weary of stories about precocious little girls. In the first place, they are themselves disagreeable and unprofitable objects of study; and in the second, they are always the precursors of a not less unprofitable middle-aged lover." (The lover in this instance is an advanced thirty-five!) — And at fifty-four he himself gives us an acute study of perhaps the most pathetically precocious little girl in English fiction. But at twenty-one, himself unsuspectingly precocious, his interest in "juvenilia," if it ever was quite normal, is magnificently held in abeyance. One gets an echo of something of this twenty years later in the grounds of Stevenson's gay complaint of James. "He cannot," writes Stevenson in "A

Humble Remonstrance," "criticise the author as he goes, 'because,' says he, comparing it with another work, '*I have been a child, but I have never been on a quest for buried treasure.*' Here is, indeed, a wilful paradox; for if he has never been on a quest for buried treasure, it can be demonstrated that he has never been a child. There never was a child (unless Master James) but has hunted gold, and been a pirate, and a military commander, and a bandit of the mountains. . . ." One cannot escape the conviction from the outset that the hidden treasure to which "Master James" surprisingly early devoted the search of a lifetime was a purely literary one. And in such a search the interruptions of juvenile Sylvias become something of a resentible impertinence.

Scarcely more than half a dozen of the novels herein reviewed are now hopelessly dead and beyond discussion; but one may read the reviews of even these with interest, for from them one gets a vivid and fresh impression of the fleeting literary fashion of a definite period. James, like any healthy young reviewer, enjoys "roasting" them. He equally enjoys, as does any reviewer worth his salt, finding specimens which he can with a clear conscience generously praise. It is the hopelessly "middling" books which one can neither magisterially excoriate nor benignantly garland which set the reviewer his most exacting and thankless task. From this last group James seems, as far as possible, to have avoided choos-

PREFACE

ing his subjects. And, rather surprisingly, it is in the first group that he seems inclined to place Anthony Trollope, three of whose works he reviews in this volume. If he grows "utterly weary" over the stories about "precocious little girls," so he evinces a temperamental disposition to weariness in taking up a novel by Trollope, that soother of sleepless bedsides and solace of infirmaries. The colloquial term "roasting" is perhaps unduly harsh for the treatment which James's few victims receive at his hands, for in general his admonitions are wrapped in a friendly wit and his disapproval phrased with a high urbanity. Nevertheless, Trollope fares rather ill with him. But he himself in his first discussion of the art of fiction, gives us, unconsciously, the reason — which is, again, youth. "Certain young persons," he gravely explains, under the cover of a presumably mature anonymity, "are often deeply concerned at their elders' interest in a book which they themselves have voted either very dull or very silly. The truth is that their elders are more credulous than they. Young persons, however they may outgrow the tendency in later life, are often more or less romancers on their own account. While the tendency lasts, they are very critical in the matter of fictions." Although this "tendency" was one which he, fortunately for us, never outgrew, time certainly mellowed and refined his judgment, notably in the case of Trollope, to whose memory he makes, in 1883, a very handsome and delicately discriminating amend, now familiar to us in "Partial Portraits."

James's treatment of Swinburne also shows us for the first time a little limitation of sympathy which, in this instance, was not to be confined to his youth but, I feel, was characteristic of his mature years. One may readily agree with all that he says of "Chastelard"; one may keenly enjoy the clear-sightedness with which he picks out its shortcomings and the neat precision with which he makes his "points"; yet one cannot fail to note that except for a final cursory sentence in his review, the play might perfectly well have been written in prose, for all that we gather from the critic. His preoccupation is with its dramatic technique, with its ineffectually solved problems of "characterization," "movement," what you will. This is, of course, wholly legitimate — up to a certain point; but, after all, the play is in verse. And to its poetry, as such, he is unexpectedly insensitive. Few men other than dilettanti, certainly few artists, have room in themselves for a reasoned appreciation of all the arts. But it is ever instructive to note their self-denials or restrictions. With James you will hunt in vain for any printed indication of a love of music. His love of the art of painting, especially of portraiture, was intense and colored many pages of his fictions. But in his long career as a critic he has given us but three deliberately reasoned studies of poets, and these three poets are French: de Musset, Gautier, and Baudelaire. It is, to me at least, singular that a master of English prose, a critic so exquisitely endowed (and so voluminous) should have left so little indication in his published writings of a love of English poetry.

But many of even his accustomed readers will find for the first time, among the following papers, Henry James's one measured excursion into the field of formal Philosophy, that family paddock in which he might well have romped with the brilliant gaiety of his eminent brother. The essay on Epictetus with its admirable discussion of Stoicism is a wholly unexpected little "James" treasure which one would not willingly have missed. As a measure, thus early, of his intellectual calibre, of his spiritual poise and sanity, of his indefeasible kinship, it assumes to the student and lover of James a value far beyond its own critical importance.

And so one might go on, discussing paper after paper in the light of his subsequent publications and detaining the reader from the real purpose of the book which is, as I said in the beginning, to be found in James's unconscious self-portraiture. It is a pleasure to share, in these resurrected pages of his, those years of his fastidiously intelligent reading and to come upon the most rewarding number of felicities of thought and of diction. But it is even more of a delight to find revealed through them the familiar features of a loved

PREFACE

author in his young prime, features already stamped with that distinguishing quality which throughout his long life never grew blurred or dimmed — his supremely endearing "fineness."

PIERRE DE CHAIGNON LA ROSE.

CAMBRIDGE, MASSACHUSETTS,
February 18, 1921.

Contents

CONTENTS

CONTENTS

NOTES AND REVIEWS

I

Fiction and Sir Walter Scott

WE opened this work with the hope of finding a general survey of the nature and principles of the subject of which it professes to treat. Its title had led us to anticipate some attempt to codify the vague and desultory canons, which cannot, indeed, be said to govern, but which in some measure define, this department of literature. We had long regretted the absence of any critical treatise upon fiction. But our regret was destined to be embittered by disappointment.

The title of the volume before us is a misnomer. The late Mr. Senior would have done better to call his book Essays on Fictions. Essays on the Novelists, even, would have been too pretentious a name. For in the first place, Mr. Senior's novelists are but five in number; and in the second, we are treated, not to an examination of their general merits, but to an exposition of the plots of their different works. These Essays, we are told, appeared in four of the leading English Reviews at intervals from the year 1821 to the year 1857. On the whole, we do not think they were worth this present resuscitation. Individually respect-

---

"Essays on Fiction." By Nassau W. Senior. London: 1864.

able enough in their time and place, they yet make a very worthless book. It is not necessarily very severe censure of a magazine article to say that it contains nothing. Sandwiched between two disquisitions of real merit, it may subsist for a couple of weeks upon the accidental glory of its position. But when half a dozen empty articles are bound together, they are not calculated to form a very substantial volume. Mr. Senior's papers may incur the fate to which we are told that inanimate bodies, after long burial, are liable on exposure to the air, — they crumble into nothing. Much better things have been said on these same authors than anything Mr. Senior has given us. Much wiser *dicta* than his lie buried in the dusty files of the minor periodicals. His remarks are but a dull restatement of the current literary criticism. He is superficial without being lively; he is indeed so heavy, that we are induced to wonder why his own weight does not force him below the surface.

But he brings one important quality to his task. He is evidently a very good novel-reader. For this alone we are grateful. By profession not a critic nor a maker of light books, he yet read novels thoughtfully. In his eyes, we fancy, the half-hour "wasted" over a work of fiction was recovered in the ensuing half-hour's meditation upon it. That Mr. Senior was indeed what is called a "confirmed" novel-reader, his accurate memory for details, his patient research into inconsistencies, — dramatic, historic, geographic, — abundantly demonstrate. The literary judgments of persons not exclusively literary are often very pleasant. There are some busy men who have read more romances and verses than twenty idle women. They have devoured all James and Dumas at odd hours. They have become thoroughly acquainted with Bulwer, Coventry Patmore, and the morning paper, in their daily transit to their place of business. They have taken advantage of a day in bed to review all Richardson. It is only because they are hardworking men that they can do these things. They do them to the great surprise of their daughters and sisters, who stay at home all day to practise listless sonatas and read the magazines. If these ladies had spent the day in teaching school, in driving bargains, or in writing sermons, they would readily do as much. For our own part, we should like nothing better than to write stories for weary lawyers and schoolmasters. Idle people are satisfied with the great romance of doing nothing. But busy people come fresh to their idleness. The imaginative faculty, which has been gasping for breath all day under the great pressure of reason, bursts forth when its possessor is once ensconced under the evening lamp, and draws a long breath in the fields of fiction. It fills its lungs for the morrow. Sometimes, we regret to say, it fills them in rather a fetid atmosphere; but for the most part it inhales the wholesome air of Anglo-Saxon good sense. Certain young persons are often deeply concerned at their elders' interest in a book which they themselves have voted either very dull or very silly. The truth is, that their elders are more credulous than they. Young persons, however they may outgrow the tendency in later life, are often more or less romancers on their own account. While the tendency lasts, they are very critical in the matter of fictions. It is often enough to damn a well-intentioned story, that the heroine should be called Kate rather than Katherine; the hero Anthony rather than Ernest. These same youthful critics will be much more impartial at middle age. Many a matron of forty will manage to squeeze out a tear over the recital of a form of courtship which at eighteen she thought absurdly improbable. She will be plunged in household cares; her life will have grown prosaic; her thoughts will have overcome their bad habits. It would seem, therefore, that as her knowledge of life has increased, her judgment of fiction, which is but a reflection of life, should have become more unerring. But it is a singular fact, that as even the most photographically disposed novels address pre-eminently the imagination, her judgment, if it be of the average weight, will remain in abeyance, while her rejuvenated imagination takes a holiday. The friends of a prolific novelist must be frequently tempted to wonder at the great man's fertility of invention, and to deprecate its moral effects. An author's wife, sitting by his study-table, and reading page after page of manuscript as he dashes it off, will not be unlikely to question him thus: "Do you never weary of this constant grinding out of false persons and events? To tell the truth, I do. I would rather not read any more, if you please. It's very pretty, but there's too much of it. It's all so untrue. I believe I will go up to the nursery. Do you never grow sick of this atmosphere of lies?" To which the prolific novelist will probably reply: "Sometimes; but not by any means so often as you might suppose. Just as the habitually busy man is the best novel-reader, so he is the best novel-writer; so the best novelist is the busiest man. It is, as you say, because I 'grind out' my men and women that I endure them. It is because I create them by the sweat of my brow that I venture to look them in the face. My *work* is my salvation. If this great army of puppets came forth at my simple bidding, then indeed I should die of their senseless clamor. But as the matter stands, they are my very good friends. The pains of labor regulate and consecrate my progeny. If it were as easy to write novels as to read them, then, too, my stomach might rebel against the phantom peopled atmosphere which I have given myself to breathe. If the novelist endowed with the greatest 'facility' ever known wrote with a tenth part of the ease attributed to him, then again his self-sufficiency might be a seventh wonder. But he

5

only half suffices to himself, and it is the constant endeavor to supply the missing half, to make both ends meet, that reconciles him to his occupation."

But we have wandered from our original proposition; which was, that the judgments of intelligent half-critics, like Mr. Senior, are very pleasant to serious critics. That is, they would be very pleasant in conversation; but they are hardly worth the trouble of reading. A person who during a long life has kept up with the light literature of his day, if he have as good a memory as Mr. Senior, will be an interesting half-hour's companion. He will remind you of a great deal that you have forgotten. This will be his principal merit. This is Mr. Senior's chief merit in the present volume.

His five authors are Scott, Bulwer, Thackeray, Mrs. Stowe, and — Colonel Senior. We are at loss to understand this latter gentleman's presence in so august a company. He wrote, indeed, a tale called "Charles Vernon", and we believe him to be a relative of the author. His presence was doubtless very good fun to the Messrs. Senior, but it is rather poor fun to the public. It must be confessed, however, that Mr. Senior has restrained the partiality of blood to decent limits. He uses his kinsman chiefly as a motive for an æsthetic dissertation of questionable soundness; and he praises his story no more than, to judge from two or three extracts, it deserves.

He begins with Sir Walter Scott. The articles

6

of which the paper on Scott is composed were
written while the Waverley Novels were in their
first editions. In our opinion this fact is their
chief recommendation. It is interesting to learn
the original effect of these remarkable books. It
is pleasant to see their classical and time-honored
figures dealt with as the latest sensations of the
year. In the year 1821, the authorship of the
novels was still unavowed. But we may gather
from several of Mr. Senior's remarks the general
tendency of the public faith. The reviewer has
several sly hits at the author of "Marmion." He
points out a dozen coincidences in the talent and
treatment of the poet and the romancer. And he
leaves the intelligent reader to draw his own conclusions. After a short preface he proceeds to the
dismemberment of each of the novels, from "Rob
Roy" downward. In retracing one by one these
long-forgotten plots and counter-plots, we yield
once more to something of the great master's
charm. We are inclined to believe that this
charm is proof against time. The popularity
which Mr. Senior celebrated forty years ago has
in no measure subsided. The only perceptible
change in Sir Walter's reputation is indeed the
inevitable lot of great writers. He has submitted
to the somewhat attenuating ordeal of classifica-
tion; he has become a standard author. He has
been provided with a seat in our literature; and
if his visible stature has been by just so much cur-
tailed, we must remember that it is only the pass-

ing guests who remain standing. Mr. Senior is a
great admirer of Sir Walter, as may be gathered
from the fact that he devotes two hundred pages
to him. And yet he has a keen eye for his defects;
and these he correctly holds to be very numerous.
Yet he still loves him in spite of his defects;
which we think will be the permanent attitude of
posterity.

Thirty years have elapsed since the publication of the last of the Waverley series. During
thirty years it has been exposed to the public
view. And meanwhile an immense deal has been
accomplished in the department of fiction. A
vast army has sprung up, both of producers and
consumers. To the latter class a novel is no longer
the imposing phenomenon it was in Sir Walter's
time. It implies no very great talent; ingenuity
is held to be the chief requisite for success. And
indeed to write a readable novel is actually a
task of so little apparent difficulty, that with
many popular writers the matter is a constant
trial of speed with the reading public. This was
very much the case with Sir Walter. His facility
in composition was almost as great as that of
Mrs. Henry Wood, of modern repute. But it
was the fashion among his critics to attribute this
remarkable fact rather to his transcendent strength
than to the vulgarity of his task. This was a wise
conviction. Mrs. Wood writes three volumes in
three months, to last three months. Sir Walter
performed the same feat, and here, after the

lapse of forty years, we still linger over those hasty pages. And we do it in the full cognizance of faults which even Mrs. Wood has avoided, of foibles for which she would blush. The public taste has been educated to a spirit of the finest discernment, the sternest exaction. No publisher would venture to offer "Ivanhoe" in the year 1864 as a novelty. The secrets of the novelist's craft have been laid bare; new contrivances have been invented; and as fast as the old machinery wears out, it is repaired by the clever artisans of the day. Our modern ingenuity works prodigies of which the great Wizard never dreamed. And besides ingenuity we have had plenty of genius. We have had Dickens and Thackeray. Twenty other famous writers are working in the midst of us. The authors of "Amyas Leigh", of "The Cloister and the Hearth", of "Romola", have all overtaken the author of "Waverley" in his own walk. Sir Edward Bulwer has produced several historical tales, which, to use an expressive vulgarism, have "gone down" very extensively. And yet old-fashioned, ponderous Sir Walter holds his own.

He was the inventor of a new style. We all know the immense advantage a craftsman derives from this fact. He was the first to sport a fashion which was eventually taken up. For many years he enjoyed the good fortune of a patentee. It is difficult for the present generation to appreciate the blessings of this fashion.

But when we review the modes prevailing for twenty years before, we see almost as great a difference as a sudden transition from the Spenserian ruff to the Byronic collar. We may best express Scott's character by saying that, with one or two exceptions, he was the first English prose story-teller. He was the first fictitious writer who addressed the public from its own level, without any preoccupation of place. Richardson is classified simply by the matter of length. He is neither a romancer nor a story-teller: he is simply Richardson. The works of Fielding and Smollett are less monumental, yet we cannot help feeling that they too are writing for an age in which a single novel is meant to go a great way. And then these three writers are emphatically preachers and moralists. In the heart of their productions lurks a didactic *raison d'être*. Even Smollett — who at first sight appears to recount his heroes' adventures very much as Leporello in the opera rehearses the exploits of Don Juan — aims to instruct and to edify. To posterity one of the chief attractions of "Tom Jones" is the fact that its author was one of the masses, that he wrote from the midst of the working, suffering mortal throng. But we feel guilty in reading the book in any such disposition of mind. We feel guilty, indeed, in admitting the question of art or science into our considerations. The story is like a vast episode in a sermon preached by a grandly humorous divine; and however we may be entertained by the way, we must not forget that our ultimate duty is to be instructed. With the minister's week-day life we have no concern: for the present he is awful, impersonal Morality; and we shall incur his severest displeasure if we view him as Henry Fielding, Esq., as a rakish man of letters, or even as a figure in English literature. "Waverley" was the first novel which was self-forgetful. It proposed simply to amuse the reader, as an old English ballad amused him. It undertook to prove nothing but facts. It was the novel irresponsible.

We do not mean to say that Scott's great success was owing solely to this, the freshness of his method. This was, indeed, of great account, but it was as nothing compared with his own intellectual wealth. Before him no prose-writer had exhibited so vast and rich an imagination: it had not, indeed, been supposed that in prose the imaginative faculty was capable of such extended use. Since Shakespeare, no writer had created so immense a gallery of portraits, nor, on the whole, had any portraits been so lifelike. Men and women, for almost the first time out of poetry, were presented in their habits as they lived. The Waverley characters were all instinct with something of the poetic fire. To our present taste many of them may seem little better than lay-figures. But there are many kinds of lay-figures. A person who goes from the workshop of a carver of figure-heads for ships to an exhibition of wax-work, will find in the latter the very reflection of nature. And even when occasionally the waxen visages are somewhat inexpressive, he can console himself with the sight of unmistakable velvet and brocade and tartan. Scott went to his prose task with essentially the same spirit which he had brought to the composition of his poems. Between these two departments of his work the difference is very small. Portions of "Marmion" are very good prose; portions of "Old Mortality" are tolerable poetry. Scott was never a very deep, intense, poetic poet: his verse alone was unflagging. So when he attacked his prose characters with his habitual poetic inspiration, the harmony of style was hardly violated. It is a great peculiarity, and perhaps it is one of the charms of his historical tales, that history is dealt with in all poetic reverence. He is tender of the past: he knows that she is frail. He certainly knows it. Sir Walter could not have read so widely or so curiously as he did, without discovering a vast deal that was gross and ignoble in bygone times. But he excludes these elements as if he feared they would clash with his numbers. He has the same indifference to historic truth as an epic poet, without, in the novels, having the same excuse. We write historical tales differently now. We acknowledge the beauty and propriety of a certain poetic reticence. But we confine it to poetry. The task of the historical story-teller is, not to invest, but to divest the past. Tennyson's "Idyls of the

King" are far more one-sided, if we may so express it, than anything of Scott's. But imagine what disclosures we should have if Mr. Charles Reade were to take it into his head to write a novel about King Arthur and his times.

Having come thus far, we are arrested by the sudden conviction that it is useless to dogmatize upon Scott; that it is almost ungrateful to criticize him. He, least of all, would have invited or sanctioned any curious investigation of his works. They were written without pretense: all that has been claimed for them has been claimed by others than their author. They are emphatically works of entertainment. As such let us cherish and preserve them. Say what we will, we should be very sorry to lose, and equally sorry to mend them. There are few of us but can become sentimental over the uncounted hours they have cost us. There are moments of high-strung sympathy with the spirit which is abroad when we might find them rather dull — in parts; but they are capital books to have read. Who would forego the companionship of all those shadowy figures which stand side by side in their morocco niches in yonder mahogany cathedral? What youth would willingly close his eyes upon that dazzling array of female forms, — so serried that he can hardly see where to choose, — Rebecca of York, Edith Plantagenet, Mary of Scotland, sweet Lucy Ashton? What maiden would consent to drop the dear acquaintance of Halbert Glendinning,

of Wilfred of Ivanhoe, of Roland Graeme and
Henry Morton? Scott was a born story-teller:
we can give him no higher praise. Surveying his
works, his character, his method, as a whole, we
can liken him to nothing better than to a strong
and kindly elder brother, who gathers his juvenile
public about him at eventide, and pours out a
stream of wondrous improvisation. Who cannot remember an experience like this? On no
occasion are the delights of fiction so intense.
Fiction? These are the triumphs of fact. In the
richness of his invention and memory, in the in-
finitude of his knowledge, in his improvidence for
the future, in the skill with which he answers, or
rather parries, sudden questions, in his low-
voiced pathos and his resounding merriment, he
is identical with the ideal fireside chronicler. And
thoroughly to enjoy him, we must again become
as credulous as children at twilight.

The only other name of equal greatness with
Scott's handled by Mr. Senior is Thackeray's.
His remarks upon Thackeray are singularly point-
less. He tells us that "Vanity Fair" is a remarkable book; but a person whose knowledge of
Thackeray was derived from Mr. Senior's article
would be surely at a loss to know wherein it is
remarkable. To him it seems to have been above
all amusing. We confess that this was not our
impression of the book on our last reading. We
remember once witnessing a harrowing melodrama
in a country playhouse, where we happened to be

seated behind a rustic young couple who labored under an almost brutal incapacity to take the play as it was meant. They were like bloodhounds on the wrong track. They laughed uproariously, whereas the great point of the piece was that they should weep. They found the horrors capital sport, and when the central horror reached its climax, their merriment had assumed such violence that the prompter, at the cost of all dramatic *vraisemblance*, had to advance to the footlights and inform them that he should be obliged to suspend the performance until betwixt them they could compose a decent visage. We can imagine some such stern inclination on the part of the author of "Vanity Fair", on learning that there were those in the audience who mistook his performance for a comedy.

We have no space to advert to Mr. Senior's observations upon Bulwer. They are at least more lenient than any we ourselves should be tempted to make. As for the article on Mrs. Stowe, it is quite out of place. It is in no sense of the word a literary criticism. It is a disquisition on the prospects of slavery in the United States.

II

Miss Prescott's "Azarian"

THE volume before us is characterized by that
venturesome, unprincipled literary spirit, de-
fiant alike of wisdom and taste, which has been
traceable through Miss Prescott's productions,
from "Sir Rohan's Ghost" downward. We looked
upon this latter work, at the time of its publication, as the very apotheosis of the picturesque;
but "Sir Rohan's Ghost", "The Amber Gods",
and even "The Rim", compared with "Azarian",
are admirably sober and coherent. Miss Prescott
has steadily grown in audacity, and in that disagreeable audacity which seems to have been fos-
tered rather by flattery than by remonstrance.
Let her pray to be delivered from her friends.

What manner of writing is it which lends itself
so frankly to aberrations of taste? It is that
literary fashion which, to speak historically, was
brought into our literature by Tennyson's poetry.
The best name for it, as a literary style, is the ideal
descriptive style. Like all founders of schools,
Tennyson has been far exceeded by his disciples.

"Azarian: an Episode." By Harriet Elizabeth Prescott.
Boston: 1864.

BY HENRY JAMES

The style in question reposes not so much upon
the observation of the objects of external nature
as the projection of one's fancy upon them. It
may be seen exemplified in its youthful vigor in
Tennyson's "Dream of Fair Women"; it is exemplified in its effete old age in Mr. Alexander
Smith and Miss Prescott, *passim*.

The writer of a work of fiction has this advantage over his critic, that he can frequently sub-
stantiate his cause by an *a posteriori* scheme of
treatment. For this reason, it is often difficult to
fasten down a story-teller to his premises, and
then to confront him with his aberrations. For
each successive delinquency he has the ready
excuse of an unimpeachable intention. Such or
such a glaring blot is the very key-stone of his
plan. When we tell Miss Prescott that some one
of her tales is marvellously void of human nature
and false to actual society, she may meet us with
the reply that a correct portraiture of nature and
society was not intended. She may claim the
poet's license. And superficially she will have the
best of it. But woe to the writer who claims
the poet's license, without being able to answer
the poet's obligations; to the writer of whatever
class who subsists upon the immunities, rather than
the responsibilities, of his task.

The subject of "Azarian" is sufficiently dramatic. A young orphan-girl—a painter of flowers
by profession — allows herself to become engaged
to a young Greek physician resident in Boston.

17

Ruth is warm-hearted and patient; Azarian is cold-hearted, selfish, and an amateur of the fine arts, especially that of flirting. He wearies of Ruth before marriage, — slights, neglects, and drives her to despair. She resolves on suicide; but when on the brink of destruction, she pauses and reconciles herself to life, and, the engagement with Azarian being broken off by tacit agreement, to happiness.

What is the central element of the above data? The element of feeling. What is the central element of the tale as it stands written? The element of words. The story contains, as it need contain, but few incidents. It is made of the stuff of a French *étude*. Its real interest lies in the history of two persons' moral intercourse. Instead of this, we are treated to an elaborate description of four persons' physical aspect and costume, and of certain aspects of inanimate nature. Of human nature there is not an unadulterated page in the book, — not a chapter of history. From beginning to end it is a succession of forced assaults upon the impregnable stronghold of painting; a wearisome series of word-pictures, linked by a slight thread of narrative, strung together, to use one of Miss Prescott's own expressions, like "beads on a leash." If the dictionary were a palette of colors, and a goose-quill a brush, Miss Prescott would be a very clever painter. But as words possess a certain inherent dignity, value, and independence, language being rather the stamped and authorized coinage which expresses the value of thought than the brute metal out of which forms are moulded, her pictures are invariably incoherent and meaningless. What do we know of Ruth and Azarian, of Charmian and Madame Saratov? Next to nothing: the little that we know we learn *in spite* of Miss Prescott's fine writing. These persons are localized, christened (we admit in rather a pagan fashion), provided with matter-of-fact occupations. They are Bostonians of the nineteenth century. The little drama in which they have parts, or something very like it, is acted every day, anywhere between the Common and the river. There is, accordingly, every presumptive reason why we should feel conscious of a certain affinity with them. But from any such sensation we are effectually debarred by Miss Prescott's inordinate fondness for the picturesque.

There is surely no principle of fictitious composition so true as this, — that an author's paramount charge is the cure of souls, to the subjection, and if need be to the exclusion, of the picturesque. Let him look to his characters: his *figures* will take care of themselves. Let the author who has grasped the heart of his purpose trust to his reader's sympathy: from that vantage-ground he may infallibly command it. In what we may call subordinate points, that is, in Miss Prescott's prominent and obtrusive points, it is an immense succor. It supplements his intention. Given an animate being, you may readily clothe it in your mind's eye with a body, a local habitation, and a name. Given we say, an animate being: that is the point. The reader who is set face to face with a gorgeous doll will assuredly fail to inspire it with sympathetic life. To do so, he must have become excited and interested. What is there in a doll to excite and interest?

In reading books of the Azarian school, — for, alas! there is a school, — we have often devoutly wished that some legal penalty were attached to the use of description. We have sighed for a novel with a *dramatis personæ* of disembodied spirits. Azarian gives his name to two hundred and fifty pages; and at the end of those pages, the chief fact with which he is associated in our minds is that he wore his hair in "waves of flaccid gold." Of Madame Saratov we read that she was the widow of a Russian exile, domesticated in Boston for the purpose of giving lessons in French, music, and Russ, and of educating her boys. In spite of the narrowness of means attributable to a lady who follows the profession of teaching, she lives in a splendor not unworthy of the Muscovite Kremlin. She has a maid to haunt her steps; her chosen raiment is silks and velvets; she sleeps in counterpanes of satin; her thimble, when she sews, is incrusted at the base with pearls; she holds a *salon*, and treats her guests to draughts of "richly-rosy" cordial. One of her dresses is a gown of green Genoa velvet, with peacock's feathers of gorgeous green and gold. What do you think of that for an exiled teacher of languages, boasting herself Russian? Perhaps, after all, it is not so improbable. In the person of Madame Saratov, Miss Prescott had doubtless the intention of a sufficiently dramatic character, — the European mistress of a *salon*. But her primary intention completely disappears beneath this thick *impasto* of words and images. Such is the fate of all her creations: either they are still-born, or they survive but for a few pages; she smothers them with caresses.

When a very little girl becomes the happy possessor of a wax-doll, she testifies her affection for it by a fond manipulation of its rosy visage. If the nose, for instance, is unusually shapely and pretty, the fact is made patent by a constant friction of the finger-tips; so that poor dolly is rapidly smutted out of recognition. In a certain sense we would compare Miss Prescott to such a little girl. She fingers her puppets to death. "Good heavens, Madam!" we are forever on the point of exclaiming, "let the poor things speak for themselves. What? are you afraid they can't stand alone?" Even the most clearly defined character would succumb beneath this repeated posing, attitudinizing, and changing of costume. Take any breathing *person* from the ranks of fiction, — Hetty in "Adam Bede", or Becky Sharp the Great (we select women advisedly, for it is known that they can endure twenty times more than men in this respect), — place her for a few pages in Miss

Prescott's charge, and what will be the result? Adieu, dear familiar friend; you melt like wax in a candle.   Imagine Thackeray forever pulling Rebecca's curls and settling the folds of her dress.

This bad habit of Miss Prescott's is more than an offence against art.   Nature herself resents it. It is an injustice to men and women to assume that the fleshly element carries such weight.   In the history of a loving and breaking heart, is that the only thing worth noticing?   Are the external signs and accidents of passion the only points to be detailed?   What we want is Passion's self, — her language, her ringing voice, her gait, the presentment of her deeds.   What do we care about the beauty of man or woman in comparison with their humanity?   In a novel we crave the spectacle of that of which we may feel that we *know* it. The only lasting fictions are those which have spoken to the reader's heart, and not to his eye; those which have introduced him to an atmosphere in which it was credible that human beings might exist, and to human beings with whom he might feel tempted to claim kinship.

When once a work of fiction may be classed as a novel, its foremost claim to merit, and indeed the measure of its merit, is its *truth*, — its truth to something, however questionable that thing may be in point of morals or of taste.   "Azarian" is true to nothing.   No one ever looked like Azarian, talked like him, nor, on the whole, acted like him; for although his specific deeds, as related in the volume before us, are few and far between, we find it difficult to believe that any one ever pursued a line of conduct so utterly meaningless as that which we are invited, or rather allowed, to attribute to him.

We have called Miss Prescott's manner the descriptive manner; but in so doing we took care to distinguish it from the famous realistic system which has asserted itself so largely in the fictitious writing of the last few years. It is not a counsel we would indiscriminately bestow, — on the contrary, we would gladly see the vulgar realism which governs the average imagination leavened by a little old-fashioned idealism, — but Miss Prescott, if she hopes to accomplish anything worth accomplishing, must renounce new-fashioned idealism for a while, and diligently study the canons of the so-called realist school. We gladly admit that she has the talent to profit by such a discipline. But to be real in writing is to describe; such is the popular notion. Were this notion correct, Miss Prescott would be a very good realist, — none better. But for this fallacious axiom we propose to substitute another, which, if it does not embrace the whole truth, comes several degrees nearer to it: to be real in writing is to express; whether by description or otherwise is of secondary importance. The short tales of M. Prosper Mérimée are eminently real; but he seldom or never describes: he conveys. It is not to be denied that the great names in the realist line are associated with a pronounced fondness for description. It is for this reason that we remind Miss Prescott of them. Let her take Balzac's "Eugénie Grandet", for instance. It will probably be affirmed that this story, the interest of which is to the full as *human* as that of her own, is equally elaborate in the painting of external objects. But such an assertion will involve a mistake: Balzac does not *paint*, does not copy, objects; his chosen instrument being a pen, he is content to *write* them. He is literally real: he presents objects as they are. The scene and persons of his drama are minutely described. Grandet's house, his sitting-room, his habits, his appearance, his dress, are all reproduced with the fidelity of a photograph. The same with Madame Grandet and Eugénie. We are exactly informed as to the young girl's stature, features, and dress. The same with Charles Grandet, when he comes upon the scene. His coat, his trousers, his watch-chain, his cravat, the curl of his hair, are all dwelt upon. We almost see the musty little sitting-room in which so much of the action goes forward. We are familiar with the gray *boiserie*, the faded curtains, the rickety card-tables, the framed samplers on the walls, Madame Grandet's foot-warmer, and the table set for the meagre dinner. And yet our sense of the human interest of the story is never lost. Why is this? It is because these things are all described *only in so far as they bear upon the action*, and not in the least for themselves. If you resolve to

24

describe a thing, you cannot describe it too carefully. But as the soul of a novel is its action, you should only describe those things which are accessory to the action. It is in determining what things *are* so accessory that real taste, science, and judgment are shown.

The reader feels that Miss Prescott describes not in accordance with any well-considered plan, but simply for the sake of describing, and of so gratifying her almost morbid love of the picturesque. There is a reason latent in every one of Balzac's tales *why* such things should appear thus, and such persons so, — a clear, well-defined reason, easily discoverable by the observing and sympathetic eye. Each separate part is conducive to the general effect; and this general effect has been studied, pondered, analyzed: in the end it is produced. Balzac lays his stage, sets his scene, and introduces his puppets. He describes them once for all; this done, the story marches. He does not linger nervously about his figures, like a sculptor about his unfinished clay-model, administering a stroke here and afixing a lump there. He has done all this beforehand, in his thoughts; his figures are completed before the story begins. This latter fact is perhaps one of the most valuable in regard to Balzac. His story exists before it is told; it stands complete before his mind's eye. It was a characteristic of his mind, enriched as it was by sensual observation, to see his figures clearly and fully as with the eye of sense. So seeing them, the desire was irresistible to present them to the reader. How clearly he saw them we may judge from the minuteness of his presentations. It was clearly done because it was *scientifically* done. That word resumes our lesson. He set down things in black and white, not, as Miss Prescott seems vaguely to aim at doing, in red, blue, and green, — in prose, scientifically, as they stood. He aimed at local color; that is, at giving the facts of things. To determine these facts required labor, foresight, reflection; but Balzac shrank from no labor of eye or brain, provided he could adequately cover the framework of his story.

Miss Prescott's style is evidently the point on which she bases her highest claims to distinction. She has been taught that, in possessing this style, she possesses a great and uncommon gift. Nothing is more false. The fine writing in which "Azarian" abounds is the cheapest writing of the day. Every magazine-story bears traces of it. It is so widely adopted, because to a person of clever fancy there is no kind of writing that is so easy, — so easy, we mean, considering the effect produced. Of course it is much easier to write in a style which necessitates no looking out of words: but such a style makes comparatively little impression. The manner in question is easy, because the writer recognizes no standard of truth or accuracy by which his performances may be measured. He does not transcribe facts, — facts must be counted, measured, weighed, which takes far too much trouble. He does not patiently study the nature and appearance of a thing until he has won from it the confession of that absolute appreciable quality, the correct statement of which is alone true description; he does not commit himself to statements, for these are dangerous things; he does not, in short, extract; he affixes. He does not consult the object to be described, so recognizing it as a fact; he consults his imagination, and so constitutes it a theme to be elaborated. In the picture which he proceeds to make, some of the qualities of the object will certainly be found; but it matters little whether they are the chief distinctive ones, — any satisfy his conscience.

All writing is narration; to describe is simply to narrate things in their order of place, instead of events in their order of time. If you consult this order, your description will stand; if you neglect it, you will have an imposing mass of words, but no recognizable *thing*. We do not mean to say that Miss Prescott has a wholly commonplace fancy. (We use the word commonplace advisedly, for there are no commonplaces so vulgar as those chromatic epigrams which mark the Tennysonian prose school.) On the contrary, she has a fancy which would serve very well to garnish a dish of solid fiction, but which furnishes poor material for the body of the dish. These clever conceits, this keen eye for the superficial picturesque, this inborn love of *bric-à-brac* and sunsets, may be made very effectively to supplement a true dramatic exposition; but they are a wretched substitute for such. And even in *bric-à-brac* and sunsets Miss Prescott's execution is crude. In her very specialty, she is but an indifferent artist. Who is so clever in the *bric-à-brac* line as M. Théophile Gautier? He takes an occasional liberty with the French language; but, on the whole, he finds his best account in a policy of studious respect even for her most irritating forms of conservatism. The consequence is, that his efforts in this line are unapproachable, and, what is better, irreproachable. One of the greatest dangers to which those who pursue this line are liable is the danger that they may fall into the ridiculous. By a close adherence to that medium of expression which other forms of thought have made respectable, this danger is effectually set at naught. What is achieved by the paternally governed French tongue may surely be effected by that chartered libertine, our own. Miss Prescott uses far too many words, synonymous words and meaningless words. Like the majority of female writers, — Mrs. Browning, George Sand, Gail Hamilton, Mrs. Stowe, — she possesses in excess the fatal gift of fluency. Her paragraphs read as if in composition she completely ignored the expedient of erasure. What painter ever painted a picture without rubbing out and transposing, displacing, effacing, replacing? There is no essential difference of system between the painting of a picture and the writing of a novel. Why should the novelist expect to do what his fellow-worker never even hopes to acquire the faculty of doing, — execute his work at a stroke? It is plain that Miss Prescott adds, tacks on, interpolates, piles up, if we may use the expression; but it seems very doubtful if she often takes counsel of the old Horatian precept, — in plain English, to scratch out. A true artist should be as sternly just as a Roman father. A moderate exercise of this Roman justice would have reduced "Azarian" to half its actual length. The various descriptive passages would have been wonderfully simplified, and we might have possessed a few good pictures.

If Miss Prescott would only take such good old English words as we possess, words instinct with the meaning of centuries, and, having fully resolved upon that which she wished to convey, cast her intention in those familiar terms which long use has invested with almost absolute force of expression, then she would describe things in a manner which could not fail to arouse the sympathy, the interest, the dormant memories of the reader. What is the possible bearing of such phrases as "vermeil ardency," or "a tang of color"? of such childish attempts at alliteration — the most frequent bugbear of Miss Prescott's readers — as "studded with starry sprinkle and spatter of splendor," and the following sentence, in which, speaking of the leaves of the blackberry-vine, she tells us that they are "damasked with deepening layer and spilth of color, brinded and barred and blotted beneath the dripping fingers of October, nipped by nest-lining bees," — and, lastly, "suffused through all their veins with the shining soul of the mild and mellow season"?

This is nothing but "words, words, words, Horatio!" They express nothing; they only seem to express. The true test of the worth of a prose description — to simplify matters we leave poetry quite out of the question — is one's ability to resolve it back into its original elements. You construct your description from a chosen object; can you, conversely, from your description construct that object? We defy any one to represent the "fine scarlet of the blackberry-vine," and "the gilded bronze of beeches," — fair sentences by themselves, which express almost as much as we can reasonably hope to express on the subject, — under the inspiration of the rhapsody above quoted, and what follows it. Of course, where so much is attempted in the way of expression, something is sometimes expressed. But with Miss Prescott such an occasional success is apt to be what the French call a *succès manqué*. This is the fault of what our authoress must allow us to call her inveterate bad taste; for whenever she has said a good thing, she invariably spoils it by trying to make it better: to let well enough alone is indeed in all respects the great lesson which experience has in store for her. It is sufficiently felicitous, for instance, as such things go, to call the chandelier

30

of a theatre "a basket of light." There stands the simple successful image. But Miss Prescott immediately tacks on the assertion that it "pours down on all its brimming burden of lustre." It would be bad taste again, if it were not such bad physiology, to speak of Azarian's flaccid hair being "drenched with some penetrating perfume, an Oriental water that stung the brain to vigor." The idea that a man's intellectual mood is at the mercy of his *pommade* is one which we recommend to the serious consideration of barbers. The reader will observe that Azarian's hair is *drenched:* an instance of the habitual intensity of Miss Prescott's style. The word *intensity* expresses better than any other its various shortcomings, or rather excesses. The only intensity worth anything in writing is intensity of thought. To endeavor to fortify flimsy conceptions by the constant use of verbal superlatives is like painting the cheeks and pencilling the eyebrows of a corpse.

Miss Prescott would rightfully resent our criticism if, after all, we had no counsel to offer. Of course our advice is to take or to leave, but it is due to ourselves to produce it.

We would earnestly exhort Miss Prescott to be *real*, to be true to something. In a notice of Mr. Charles Reade recently published in the *Atlantic*, our authoress indulged in a fling at Mr. Anthony Trollope for what she probably considers his grovelling fidelity to minute social truths. But we hold it far better to be real as Mr. Trollope is real, than to be ideal after the fashion of the authoress of "Azarian." As in the writing of fiction there is no grander instrument than a potent imagination, such as Mr. Hawthorne's, for instance, so there is no more pernicious dependence than an unbridled fancy. Mr. Trollope has not the imagination of Mr. Reade, his strong grasp of the possible; but he has a delicate perception of the actual which makes every whit as firm ground to work upon. This delicate perception of the actual Miss Prescott would do well to cultivate: if Mr. Trollope is too distasteful to her, she may cultivate it in the attentive perusal of Mr. Reade, in whom there are many Trollopes. Let her not fear to grovel, but take note of what is, constitute herself an observer, and review the immeasurable treasures she has slighted. If she will conscientiously do this, she will need to invent neither new and unprecedented phases of humanity nor equally unprecedented nouns and adjectives. There are already more than enough for the novelist's purpose. All we ask of him is to use the material ready to his hand. When Miss Prescott reconciles herself to this lowly task, *then* and then only will she find herself truly rich in resource.

III
Lindisfarn Chase

THIS is a fair specimen of a second-rate novel, a species of work which commands a certain degree of respect; for second-rate novels are the great literary feature of the day. It is the work of a man who has no vocation for his task except a well-practised hand, and who would yet find it very hard that he should not write his novel with the rest. In the present condition of literature, when novel-writing is at once a trade and a past-time, books of this class are inevitable. Let us take them for what they are worth. Both in England and in this country they find an immense public of excellent persons, whose chief delight in literature is the contemplation of respectable mediocrity. Such works as "Lindisfarn Chase" are plentiful, because they are so easy to write; they are popular, because they are so easy to read.

To compose a novel on the model before us, one must have seen a good many well-bred people, and have read a good many well-written novels. These qualifications are easily acquired. The novel of a writer who possesses them will be (if it

"Lindisfarn Chase." By T. Adolphus Trollope. New York: 1864.

is successful) a reflection of the manner of his social equals or inferiors and of his literary superiors. If it is unsuccessful, the reason will probably be that the author has sought inspiration in his social superiors. In the case of an attempted portraiture of a lower order of society, a series of false representations will not be so likely to prove fatal, because the critics and the reading public are not so well informed as to the facts. A book like "Lindisfarn Chase" might almost be written by recipe; so much depends upon the writer's familiarity with good society, and upon his good taste; so little depends upon his real dramatic perception. The first requisite is to collect a large number of persons, so many that you have no space to refine upon individuals, even if you should sometimes feel dangerously tempted to do so; to give these persons pleasant, expressive names, and to scatter among them a few handfuls of clever description. The next step is to make a fair distribution of what may be called pre-historic facts, — facts which are referred to periods prior to the opening of the tale, and which serve, as it were, as your base of supplies during its progress. According as these facts are natural and commonplace, or improbable and surprising, your story is an ordinary novel of manners, a sober photograph of common life, or a romance. Their great virtue is to relieve the writer of all analysis of character, to enable him to forge his interest out of the exhibition of circumstance rather than out of the examination of motive. The work before us affords an instance to the point.

Mr. Trollope desires to represent a vicious and intriguing young girl; so he takes an English maiden, and supposes her to have been educated in Paris. Vice and intrigue are conjured up by a touch of the pen. Paris covers a multitude of sins. Mr. Trollope fills his young lady's mouth with French phrases and allusions, assures us that she was a very hard case, and lo! she does service as a complex human creature. Margaret Lindisfarn is a weak repetition of Thackeray's Blanche Amory. *Heu quanto minus!* Mr. Trollope is very far from possessing even his brother's knowledge of the workings of young girls' hearts. Young girls are seldom so passionless as Margaret Lindisfarn. Beautiful, wealthy, still in her teens, she is represented as possessing the deep diplomatic heart of an old gentlewoman who has half a dozen daughters on her hands. But granting that it is possible that she should be as coldly selfish as she is made out to be, why refer it all to Paris? It is surely not necessary to have lived in Paris to be heartless. Margaret is full of grace and tact, and is always well-dressed: a residence in the French capital may have been required to explain these advantages. She is cold-hearted, scheming, and has her beautiful eyes perpetually fastened upon the main chance. We see no reason why these attributes should not have been of insular growth.

NOTES AND REVIEWS

The only definite character we are able to assign to the book is that of an argument against educating English youth in Paris. A paltry aim, the reader may say, for a work of art of these dimensions. He will say truly: but from such topics as this is the English fiction of the present day glad to draw inspiration.

BY HENRY JAMES

IV

Emily Chester: A Novel

THIS book is so well-meaning, that we are deterred by a feeling of real consideration for its author from buying back, in the free expression of our regret at misused time, the several tedious hours we have spent over its pages. It is emphatically a dull work; and yet it is a work in which many persons might discern that archopponent of dulness, — a questionable moral tendency. It is almost, we think, a worthless book; and yet it is decidedly a serious one. Its composition has evidently been a great matter for the author.

This latter fact commands our sympathy and tempers our severity; and yet at the same time it arouses a strong feeling of melancholy. This is the age of conscientious poor books, as well as of unscrupulous clever ones; and we are often appalled at the quantity of ponderous literary matter which is kept afloat in the market by the simple fact that those who have set it afloat are persons of a well-meaning sort. When a book is both bad

"Emily Chester." [By Mrs. A. M. C. Seemuller.] Boston: 1864.

37

and clever, the critic who pulls it to pieces feels that the author has some consolation in the sweetness of his own wit for the acerbity of that of others. But when a book is destitute of even the excellence of a pleasant style, it is surrounded with an atmosphere of innocence and innocuousness which inspires the justly indignant reviewer with compassion for the hapless adventurer who has nothing to fall back upon.

We have called "Emily Chester" a dull book, because the author has chosen a subject and a manner alike certain to make it dull in any but the most skilful hands. She has told a story of character in a would-be psychological mode; not of every-day character, such as is employed by Mr. Trollope and Miss Austen, but of character which she must allow us to term exceptional. She has brought together three persons; for although in the latter part of the book other names occur with some frequency, they remain nothing but names; and during three hundred and fifty close pages, we are invited to watch the moral operations of this romantic trio. What a chance for dulness is here!

She has linked her three persons together by a simple dramatic mechanism. They are a husband, a wife, and a lover. Emily Chester, the wife, is a beautiful and accomplished young woman. When we have said this, we have said as much about her as we venture positively to assert; for any further acquaintance with her is the result of mere guesswork. Her person is minutely described. At eighteen she has a magnificently developed figure. We are told that she has a deep sense of the beautiful; we gather generally that she is good yet proud, — with a stern Romanesque pride, — passionate yet cold, and although very calm and stately on all occasions, quite free from petty feminine affectations; that she is furthermore earnestly devoted to music, and addicted to quoting from the German. Is she clever? We know not. The author has evidently intended to make her very perfect, but she has only succeeded in making her very inane. She behaves on all occasions in a most irreproachable, inhuman manner; as if from the hour of her birth she had resolved to be a martyr, and was grimly determined not to be balked of her purpose. When anything particularly disagreeable happens, she becomes very pale and calm and statuesque. Although in the ordinary affairs of life she is sufficiently cheerful and voluble, whenever anything occurs a little out of the usual way she seems to remember the stake and the torture, and straightway becomes silent and cold and classical. She goes down into her grave after a life of acute misery without ever having "let on", as the phrase is, that there has been anything particular the matter with her. In view of these facts, we presume that the author has aimed at the creation of a perfect woman, — a woman high-toned, high-spirited, high-souled, high-bred, high and mighty in all respects.

Heaven preserve us from any more radical specimens of this perfection!

To wish to create such a specimen was a very laudable, but a very perilous ambition; to have created it, would have been an admirable achievement. But the task remains pretty much what it was. Emily Chester is not a character; she is a mere shadow; the mind's eye strives in vain to body her forth from the fluent mass of talk in which she is embodied. We do not wish to be understood as attributing this fact of her indistinctness to the fact of her general excellence and nobleness; good women, thank heaven, may be as vividly realized as bad ones. We attribute it to the want of clearness in the author's conception, to the want of science in her execution.

Max Crampton and Frederick Hastings, who are both very faulty persons, are equally incomplete and intangible. Max is an eccentric millionnaire, a mute adorer of Miss Chester; mute, that is, with regard to his passion, but a great talker and theorizer on things in general. We have a strong impression of having met him before. He is the repetition of a type that has of late years obtained great favor with lady novelists: the ugly, rich, middle-aged lover, with stern brows and white teeth; reticent and yet ardent; indolent and yet muscular, full of satire and commonsense. Max is partly a German, as such men often are, in novels. In spite of these striking characteristics, his fine rich ugliness, his sardonic laugh, his enormous mental strength, the fulness of his devotion and of his magnanimity, he is anything but a living, moving person. He is essentially a woman's man; one of those impossible heroes, whom lady novelists concoct half out of their own erratic fancies and half out of those of other lady novelists. But if Max is a woman's man, what is Frederick Hastings? He is worse; he is almost a man's woman. He is nothing; he is more shadowy even than Emily. We are told that he had beauty and grace of person, delicacy, subtlety of mind, womanly quickness of perception. But, like his companions, he utterly fails to assert himself.

Such are the three mutually related individuals with whom we are brought into relation. We cannot but suppose that, as we have said, the author intended them for persons of exceptional endowments. Such beauty, such moral force and fervor, as are shadowed forth in Emily; so sublime and Gothic an ugliness, such intellectual depth, breadth, strength, so vast an intellectual and moral capacity generally, as we are taught to associate with Max: these traits are certainly not vouchsafed to the vulgar many. Nor is it given to one man out of five thousand, we apprehend, to be so consummate a charmer as Frederick Hastings.

But granting the existence of these almost unique persons, we recur to our statement that they are treated in a psychological fashion. We use this word, for want of a better one, in what we may call its technical sense. We apply it to the fact that the author makes the action of her story rest, not only exclusively, but what is more to the point, avowedly, upon the temperament, nature, constitution, instincts, of her characters; upon their physical rather than upon their moral sense. There is a novel at present languidly circulating in our literature — "Charles Auchester" — which is generally spoken of by its admirers as a "novel of temperament." "Emily Chester" is of the same sort; it is an attempt to exalt the physical sensibilities into the place of monitors and directors, or at any rate to endow them with supreme force and subtlety. Psychology, it may be said, is the observation of the moral and intellectual character. We repeat that we use the word in what we have called its technical sense, the scrutiny, in fiction, of *motive* generally. It is very common now-a-days for young novelists to build up figures *minus* the soul. There are two ways of so eliminating the spiritual principle. One is by effectually diluting it in the description of outward objects, as is the case with the picturesque school of writing; another is by diluting it in the description of internal subjects. This latter course has been pursued in the volume before us. In either case the temperament is the nearest approach we have to a soul. Emily becomes aware of Frederick Hastings's presence at Mrs. Dana's party by "a species of animal magnetism." Many writers would have said by the use of her eyes. During the period of her grief at her father's death, Max feels that he is "constitutionally powerless" to help her. So he does not even try. As she regains her health, after her marriage, "her morbid sensitiveness to outward influences" returns with renewed vigor. Her old constitutional repulsion towards (*sic*) her husband increases with fearful rapidity. She tries in vain to overcome it: "the battle with, and denial of, instinct resulted as such conflicts inevitably must." The mood in which she drives him from her, in what may not be inappropriately termed the "balcony scene" on the Lake of Como, arises from her having been "true to her constitutional sensitiveness." Max recognizes the old friendship between his wife and Hastings to have been the "constitutional harmony of two congenial natures." Emily's spirit, on page 245, is bound by "human law with which its nature had no correspondence." We are told on page 285, that Frederick Hastings held Emily fascinated by his "motive power over the supersensuous portion of her being."

But it is needless to multiply examples. There is hardly a page in which the author does not insinuate her conviction that, in proportion as a person is finely organized, in so far is he apt to be the slave of his instincts, — the subject of unaccountable attractions and repulsions, loathings and yearnings. We do not wish to use hard words; perhaps, indeed, the word which is in our mind,

43

and which will be on the lips of many, is in these latter days no longer a hard word; but if "Emily Chester" is immortal, it is by the fact of the above false representation. It is not in making a woman prefer another man to her husband, nor even in making her detest a kind and virtuous husband. It is in showing her to be so disposed without an assignable reason; it is in making her irresponsible. But the absurdity of such a view of human nature nullifies its pernicious tendency. Beasts and idiots act from their instincts; educated men and women, even when they most violate principle, act from their reason, however perverted, and their affections, however misplaced.

We presume that our author wishes us to admire, or at least to compassionate, her heroine; but we must deny her the tribute of either sentiment. It may be claimed for her that she was ultimately victorious over her lawless impulses; but this claim we reject. Passion was indeed conquered by duty, but life was conquered by passion. The true victory of mind would have been, not perhaps in a happy, but at least in a peaceful life. Granting the possibility of Emily's having been beset by these vague and nameless conflicting forces, the one course open to her was to conquer a peace. Women who love less wisely than well engage our sympathy even while we deny them our approbation; but a woman who indulges in a foolish passion, without even the excuse of loving well, must be curtly and sternly dismissed.

At no period of Emily's history could she have
assigned a reason to herself (let alone her disabil-
ity to make her position clear to her husband)
for her intense loathing of Max Crampton! We
do not say that she could not have defended her
position; she could not have even indicated it.
Nor could she have given a name to the state of
her feelings with regard to Hastings. She admits
to herself that he does not engage her heart; he
dominates merely "the supersensuous portion of
her being." We hope that this glittering gener-
ality was not of Emily's own contrivance. Sore
distressed indeed must she have been, if she could
not have made herself out a better case than her
biographer has made for her. If her biographer
had represented her as *loving* Frederick Hastings,
as struggling with her love, and finally reducing
it from a disorderly to an orderly passion, we
should have pledged her our fullest sympathy and
interest. Having done so well, we might have
regretted that she should not have done better,
and have continued to adorn that fashionable
society of which she was so brilliant a member.
She was in truth supremely handsome; she might
have lived for her beauty's sake. But others have
done so much worse, that we should have been
sorry to complain. As the case stands, we complain bitterly, not so much of Emily as of the
author; for we are satisfied that an Emily is impossible. Even from the author's point of view,
however, her case is an easy one. She had no

hate to contend with, merely loathing; no love, merely yearning; no feelings, as far as we can make out, merely sensations. Except the loss of her property, we maintain that she has no deep sorrow in life, She refuses Hastings in the season of her trial. Good: she would not marry a man whom she did not love, merely for a subsistence; so far she was an honest woman. But she refuses him at the cost of a great agony. We do not understand her predicament. It is our belief that there is no serious middle state between friendship and love. If Emily did not love Hastings, why should she have suffered so intensely in refusing him? Certainly not out of sympathy for him disappointed. We may be told that she did not love him in a way to marry him: she loved him, then, as a mother or a sister. The refusal of his hand must have been, in such a case, an easy rather than a difficult task. She accepts Max as irresponsibly as she refuses Frederick, — because there is a look in his eyes of claiming her body and soul, "through his divine right of the stronger." Such a look must be either very brutal or very tender. What we know of Max forbids us to suppose that in his case it was tainted with the former element; it must accordingly have expressed the ripened will to serve, cherish, and protect. Why, then, should it in later years, as Emily looked back upon it, have filled her with so grisly a horror? Such terrors are self-made. A woman who despises her husband's person may perhaps, if she is very weak and nervous, grow to invest it with numerous fantastic analogies. If, on the contrary, she is as admirably self-poised as Mrs. Crampton, she will endeavor, by the steady contemplation of his magnificent intellect and his generous devotion, to discern the subtle halo (always discernible to the eye of belief) which a noble soul sheds through an ignoble body. Our author will perhaps resent our insinuation that the unutterable loathing of Max's wife for him was anything so easily disposed of as a contempt for his person. Such a feeling is a very lawful one; it may easily be an impediment to a wife's happiness; but when it is balanced by so deep a conviction of her partner's moral and intellectual integrity as Mrs. Crampton's own mental acuteness furnished her, it is certainly not an insuperable bar to a career of comfortable resignation. When it assumes the unnatural proportions in which it is here exhibited, it conclusively proves that its subject is a profoundly vicious person. Emily found just that in Hastings which she missed in her husband. If the absence of this quality in Max was sufficient to unfit him for her true love, why should not its presence have been potent enough to insure her heart to Frederick? We doubt very much whether she had a heart; we mistrust those hearts which are known only by their ineffable emptiness and woe. But taking her biographer's word for it that she had, the above little piece of

logic ought, we think, effectually to confound it.
Heart-histories, as they are called, have generally
been considered a very weary and unprofitable
species of fiction; but we infinitely prefer the old-
fashioned love-stories, in which no love but heart-
love was recognized, to these modern teachings of
a vagrant passion which has neither a name nor
a habitation. We are not particularly fond of
any kind of sentimentality; but Heaven defend
us from the sentimentality which soars above all
our old superstitions, and allies itself with anything so rational as a theory.

BY HENRY JAMES

V

Miss Alcott's "Moods"

UNDER the above title, Miss Alcott has given us her version of the old story of the husband, the wife, and the lover. This story has been told so often that an author's only pretext for telling it again is his consciousness of an ability to make it either more entertaining or more instructive; to invest it with incidents more dramatic, or with a more pointed moral. Its interest has already been carried to the furthest limits, both of tragedy and comedy, by a number of practised French writers: under this head, therefore, competition would be superfluous. Has Miss Alcott proposed to herself to give her story a philosophical bearing? We can hardly suppose it.

We have seen it asserted that her book claims to deal with the "doctrine of affinities." What the doctrine of affinities is, we do not exactly know; but we are inclined to think that our author has been somewhat maligned. Her book is, to our perception, innocent of any doctrine whatever.

The heroine of "Moods" is a fitful, wayward, and withal most amiable young person, named Sylvia. We regret to say that Miss Alcott takes

---

"Moods." By Louisa M. Alcott. Boston: 1865.

49

her up in her childhood. We are utterly weary of stories about precocious little girls. In the first place, they are in themselves disagreeable and unprofitable objects of study; and in the second, they are always the precursors of a not less unprofitable middle-aged lover. We admit that, even to the middle-aged, Sylvia must have been a most engaging little person. One of her means of fascination is to disguise herself as a boy and work in the garden with a hoe and wheelbarrow; under which circumstances she is clandestinely watched by one of the heroes, who then and there falls in love with her. Then she goes off on a camping-out expedition of a week's duration, in company with three gentlemen, with no superfluous luggage, as far as we can ascertain, but a cockle-shell stuck "pilgrim-wise" in her hat. It is hard to say whether the impropriety of this proceeding is the greater or the less from the fact of her extreme youth. This fact is at any rate kindly overlooked by two of her companions, who become desperately enamored of her before the week is out. These two gentlemen are Miss Alcott's heroes. One of them, Mr. Geoffrey Moor, is unobjectionable enough; we shall have something to say of him hereafter: but the other, Mr. Adam Warwick, is one of our oldest and most inveterate foes. He is the inevitable *cavaliere servente* of the precocious little girl; the laconical, satirical, dogmatical lover, of about thirty-five, with the "brown mane", the "quiet smile", the

"masterful soul", and the "commanding eye."
Do not all novel-readers remember a figure, a
hundred figures, analogous to this? Can they
not, one of his properties being given, — the
"quiet smile" for instance, — reconstruct the
whole monstrous shape? When the "quiet smile"
is suggested, we know what is coming: we foresee
the cynical bachelor or widower, the amateur of
human nature, "Full of strange oaths, and bearded
like the pard", who has travelled all over the world,
lives on a mysterious patrimony, and spends his
time in breaking the hearts and the wills of de-
mure little school-girls, who answer him with
"Yes, sir", and "No, sir."

Mr. Warwick is plainly a great favorite with
the author. She has for him that affection which
writers entertain, not for those figures whom they
have well known, but for such as they have much
pondered. Miss Alcott has probably mused upon
Warwick so long and so lovingly that she has lost
all sense of his proportions. There is a most dis-
couraging good-will in the manner in which lady
novelists elaborate their impossible heroes. There
are, thank Heaven, no such men at large in society.
We speak thus devoutly, not because Warwick is
a vicious person, — on the contrary, he exhibits
the sternest integrity; but because, apparently as
a natural result of being thoroughly conscientious,
he is essentially disagreeable. Women appear to
delight in the conception of men who shall be in-
supportable to men. Warwick is intended to be

a profoundly serious person. A species of prologue is prefixed to the tale, in which we are initiated into his passion for one Ottila, a beautiful Cuban lady. This chapter is a literary curiosity. The relations of the two lovers are illustrated by means of a dialogue between them. Considering how bad this dialogue is, it is really very good. We mean that, considering what nonsense the lovers are made to talk, their conversation is quite dramatic. We are not certain of the extent to which the author sympathizes with her hero; but we are pretty sure that she has a secret "Bravo" in store for him upon his exit. He talks to his mistress as no sane man ever talked to a woman. It is not too much to say that he talks like a brute. Ottila's great crime has been, that, after three months' wooing, he has not found her so excellent a person as he at first supposed her to be. This is a specimen of his language: "You allured my eye with loveliness, my ear with music; piqued curiosity, pampered pride, and subdued will by flatteries subtly administered. Beginning afar off, you let all influences do their work, till the moment came for the effective stroke. Then you made a crowning sacrifice of maiden modesty, and owned you loved me." What return does she get for the sacrifice, if sacrifice it was? To have her favors thrown back in her teeth on the day that her lover determines to jilt her. To jilt a woman in an underhand fashion is bad enough; but to break your word to her and at the same time load her with outrage, to call her evil names because she is so provokingly in the right, to add the foulest insult to the bitterest injury, — these things may be worthy of a dissolute adventurer, but they are certainly not worthy of a model hero. Warwick tells Ottila that he is "a man untamed by any law but that of [his] own will." He is further described as "violently virtuous, a masterful soul, bent on living out his aspirations at any cost"; and as possessed of "great nobility of character, great audacity of mind"; as being "too fierce an iconoclast to suit the old party, too individual a reformer to join the new", and "a grand man in the rough, an excellent tonic for those who have courage to try him." Truly, for her courage in trying him, poor Ottila is generously rewarded. His attitude towards her may be reduced to this: — Three months ago, I fell in love with your beauty, your grace, your wit. I took them as a promise of a moral elevation which I now find you do not possess. And yet, the deuse take it, I am engaged to you. *Ergo*, you are false, immodest, and lacking in the "moral sentiment", and I will have nothing to do with you. I may be a sneak, a coward, a brute; but at all events, I am untamed by any law, etc.

Before the picnic above mentioned is over, Warwick and Moor have, unknown to each other, both lost their hearts to Sylvia. Warwick may not declare himself, inasmuch as, to do him justice, he considers himself bound by word to the unfortunate beauty of the Havana. But Moor, who is free to do as he pleases, forthwith offers himself. He is refused, the young girl having a preference for Warwick. But while she is waiting for Warwick's declaration, his flirtation with Ottila comes to her knowledge. She recalls Moor, marries him, and goes to spend her honeymoon among the White Mountains. Here Warwick turns up. He has been absent in Cuba, whether taking back his rude speeches to Ottila, or following them up with more of the same sort, we are not informed. He is accordingly ignorant of the change in his mistress's circumstances. He finds her alone on the mountain-side, and straightway unburdens his heart. Here ensues a very pretty scene, prettily told. On learning the sad truth, Warwick takes himself off, over the crest of the hill, looking very tall and grand against the sun, and leaving his mistress alone in the shadow. In the shadow she passes the rest of her brief existence. She might have lived along happily enough, we conceive, masquerading with her gentle husband in the fashion of old days, if Warwick had not come back, and proffered a visit, — his one natural and his one naughty act. Of course it is all up with Sylvia. An honest man in Warwick's position would immediately have withdrawn, on seeing that his presence only served seriously to alienate his mistress from her husband. A dishonest man would have remained and made love to his friend's wife.

Miss Alcott tries to persuade us that her hero does neither; but we maintain that he adopts the latter course, and, what is worse, does it like an arrant hypocrite. He proceeds to lay down the law of matrimonial duty to Sylvia in a manner which, in our opinion, would warrant her in calling in her husband to turn him out of the house. He declares, indeed, that he designs no "French sentiment nor sin", whatever these may be; but he exerts the utmost power of his "masterful soul" to bully her into a protest against her unnatural union. No man with any sense of decency, no man of the slightest common-sense, would presume to dogmatize in this conceited fashion upon a matter with which he has not the least concern. Miss Alcott would tell us, we presume, that it is not as a lover, but as a friend, that Warwick offers the advice here put into his mouth. Family friends, when they know what they are about, are only too glad to shirk the responsibility of an opinion in matrimonial differences. When a man beats, starves, or otherwise misuses his wife, any judicious acquaintance will take the responsibility of advising the poor woman to seek legal redress; and he need not, to use Miss Alcott's own preposition, have an affinity "for" her, to do so. But it is inconceivable that a wise and virtuous gentleman should deliberately persuade two dear friends — dear equally to himself and to each other — to pick imperceptible flaws in a relation whose inviolability is the great interest of their lives, and which, from the picture presented to us, is certainly one of exceptional comfort and harmony.

In all this matter it strikes us that Sylvia's husband is the only one to be pitied. His wife, while in a somnambulistic state, confesses the secret of her illicit affection. Moor is, of course, bitterly outraged, and his anger is well described. Sylvia pities him intensely, but insists with sweet inflexibility that she cannot continue to be his wife, and dismisses him to Europe, with a most audacious speech about the beautiful eternity and the immortality of love. Moor, who for a moment has evinced a gleam of natural passion, which does something towards redeeming from ludicrous unreality the united efforts of the trio before us, soon recovers himself, and submits to his fate precisely like a morbidly conscientious young girl who is engaged in the formation of her character under the direction of her clergyman. From this point accordingly the story becomes more and more unnatural, although, we cheerfully add, it becomes considerably more dramatic, and is much better told. All this portion is, in fact, very pretty; indeed, if it were not so essentially false, we should call it very fine. As it is, we can only use the expression in its ironical sense. Moor consents to sacrifice himself to the beautiful ethical abstraction which his wife and her lover have concocted between them. He will go to Europe and await the dawning of some new abstraction, under whose starry influence he may return. When he does return, it will not be, we may be sure, to give his wife the thorough rating she deserves.

At the eleventh hour, when the vessel is about to start, Warwick turns up, and thrusts himself, as a travelling companion, upon the man he has outraged. As Warwick was destined to die a violent death, we think Miss Alcott might have here appropriately closed her book by making Moor pitch Adam into the water for his impertinence. But as usual, Warwick has his own way.

During their absence, Sylvia sinks into a rapid decline. After a certain interval they start homeward. But their ship is wrecked; Warwick is lost in trying to save Moor's life; and Moor reaches home alone. Sylvia then proceeds to put him and every one else in the wrong by dying the death of the righteous.

The two most striking facts with regard to "Moods" are the author's ignorance of human nature, and her self-confidence in spite of this ignorance. Miss Alcott doubtless knows men and women well enough to deal successfully with their every-day virtues and temptations, but not well enough to handle great dramatic passions. The consequence is, that her play is not a real play, nor her actors real actors.

But beside these facts are others, less salient perhaps, upon which it is pleasanter to touch. Chief among these is the author's decided cleverness; that quality to which we owe it that, in spite of the absurdities of the action, the last half of her book is replete with beauty and vigor. What shall we call this quality? Imagination does not seem to us too grand a word. For, in the absence of knowledge, our authoress has derived her figures, as the German derived his camel, from the depths of her moral consciousness. If they are on this account the less real, they are also on this account the more unmistakably instinct with a certain beauty and grace. If Miss Alcott's experience of human nature has been small, as we should suppose, her admiration for it is nevertheless great. Putting aside Adam's treatment of Ottila, she sympathizes throughout her book with none but great things. She has the rare merit, accordingly, of being very seldom puerile. For inanimate nature, too, she has a genuine love, together with a very pretty way of describing it. With these qualities there is no reason why Miss Alcott should not write a very good novel, provided she will be satisfied to describe only that which she has seen. When such a novel comes, as we doubt not it eventually will, we shall be among the first to welcome it. With the exception of two or three celebrated names, we know not, indeed, to whom, in this country, unless to Miss Alcott, we are to look for a novel above the average.

VI

The Noble School of Fiction

MR. HENRY KINGSLEY may be fairly described as a reduced copy of his brother. He lacks, indeed, many of his brother's gifts; especially that tone of authority which the Rev. Charles Kingsley derives from his connection with the Church and the University. He cherishes, publicly, at least, no original theory of history. He has less talent, to begin with; and less knowledge, to end with. But he is nevertheless, as perhaps indeed for these very reasons, a capital example of the pure Kingsley spirit. In him we see the famous muscular system of morality presented in its simplest form, disengaged from the factitious graces of scholarship. Our feeling for Mr. Henry Kingsley, for which under other circumstances we could not positively vouch, is almost kindled into gratitude when we consider the good service he has rendered the rising generation in divesting the name of Kingsley of its terror. As long as Mr. Charles Kingsley wrote about the age of Elizabeth and the age of Hypatia, and exercised his powerful and perverse

---

"The Hillyars and the Burtons: a Story of Two Families." By Henry Kingsley. Boston: 1865.

imagination upon the Greeks of the fifth century and the Englishmen of the sixteenth, those young persons who possessed only the common-school notions of the rise of Protestantism and the fall of Paganism had nothing to depend upon during their slow convalescence from the Kingsley fever — which we take to be a malady natural to youth, like the measles or the scarlatina, leaving the subject much stronger and sounder — but a vague uncomfortable sensation of the one-sidedness of their teacher. Those persons, on the other hand, who had inquired for themselves into the manners of the Elizabethan era, discovered, what they had all along expected, that both Mr. Kingsley's Englishmen and his Spaniards, although in a certain way wonderfully life-like, were yet not the characters of history; that these persons were occupied with far other thoughts than that of *posing* for the confusion of the degenerate Anglo-Saxons of the present day; that they were infinitely brutal, indeed, and sentimental in their own fashion; but that this fashion was very unlike Mr. Kingsley's. There is a way of writing history which on general grounds impugns the writer's fidelity; that is, studying it with a prejudice either in favor of human nature or against it. This is the method selected by Mr. Kingsley and Mr. Carlyle. Mr. Kingsley's prejudice is, on the whole, in favor of human nature; while Mr. Carlyle's is against it. It is astonishing, however, how nearly the two writers coincide in their conclusions. When in

"Two Years Ago" Mr. Charles Kingsley took up the men and women about us, he inflicted upon his cause an injury which his brother's novels have only served to aggravate. He made a very thrilling story; a story which we would advise all young persons to read, as they take a cold bath in winter time, for the sake of the "reaction"; but he forfeited his old claim to being considered a teacher. He gave us the old giants and the old cravens; but giants and cravens were found to be insufficient to the demands of the age. The age has stronger muscles and weaker nerves than Mr. Kingsley supposes.

The author of the volume before us tells us in a brief preface that his object has been to paint the conflict between love and duty in the breast of an uneducated girl, who, after a year and a half at boarding-school, "might have developed into a very noble lady." He adds that this question of the claims of duty as opposed to love is one which, "thanks to the nobleness of *our* women", is being continually put before us. To what women the possessive pronoun refers is left to conjecture: but judging from the fact that whenever the Messrs. Kingsley speak of the human race in general they mean their own countrymen in particular, we may safely apply it to the daughters of England. But however this may be, the question in point is one which, in spite of Mr. Kingsley's preface, and thanks to his incompetency to tell a straight story, is *not* put before us here. We are treated to nothing so beautiful, so simple, or so interesting. Does the author really believe that any such severe intention is discernible among his chaotic, inartistic touches? We can hardly think that he does; and yet, if he does not, his preface is inconceivably impudent. It is time that this fashion were done away with, of tacking a subject upon your story on the eve of publication. As long as Mr. Kingsley's book has a subject, what matters it whether it be outside of the story or inside? The story is composed on the plan of three-fourths of the modern popular novels. The author leaps astride of a half-broken fancy, starts off at a brisk trot (we are all familiar with the cheerful energetic colloquy or description with which these works open), and trusts to Providence for the rest. His main dependence is his command of that expedient which is known in street parlance as "collecting a crowd." He overawes the reader by the force of numbers; and in this way he is never caught *solus* upon the stage; for to be left alone with his audience, or even to be forced into a prolonged *tête-à-tête* with one of his characters, is the giant terror of the second-rate novelist. Another unfailing resource of Mr. Henry Kingsley is his intimate acquaintance with Australian life. This fact is evidently in his opinion, by itself, almost a sufficient outfit for a novelist. It is one of those rudimentary truths which cannot be too often repeated, that to write a novel it is not necessary to have been a traveller, an adventurer, a sight-seer; it is simply necessary to be an artist. Mr. Kingsley's descriptions of Australia are very pretty; but they are not half so good as those of Mr. Charles Reade, who, as far as we know, has never visited the country. We mean that they do not give the reader that vivid impression of a particular place which the genius of Mr. Reade contrives to produce. Mr. Reade went to Aus-tralia — that is, his imagination went — on pur-pose to compose certain chapters in "Never too Late to Mend." Mr. Kingsley went in the flesh; but Mr. Kingsley in the flesh is not equal to Mr. Reade in the spirit.

The main object of the novels of Mr. Charles Kingsley and his brother has seemed to us to be to give a strong impression of what they would call "human nobleness." Human nobleness, when we come across it in life, is a very fine thing; but it quite loses its flavor when it is made so cheap as it is made in these works. It is em-phatically an occasional quality; it is not, and, with all due respect for the stalwart Englishmen of Queen Elizabeth's time and eke of Queen Vic-toria's, it never was the prime element of human life, nor were its headquarters at any time on the island of Great Britain. By saying it is an occa-sional quality, we simply mean that it is a great one, and is therefore manifested in great and exceptional moments. In the ordinary course of life it does not come into play; it is sufficiently represented by courage, modesty, industry. Let the novelist give us these virtues for what they are, and not for what no true lover of human nature would have them pretend to be, or else let him devise sublime opportunities, situations which really match the latent nobleness of the human soul. We can all of us take the outside view of magnanimity; it belongs to the poet to take the inside one. It seems to us that the sturdy and virtuous Burtons in the present tale have but a narrow scale of emotions. Mr. Kingsley would apparently have us look upon them all as heroes, which, with the best will in the world, we cannot succeed in doing. A hero is but a species of genius, a genius *pro tempore*. The Burtons are essentially commonplace. The best that can be said of them is that they had a good notion of their duty. It is here, as it seems to us, that praise should begin, and not, as Mr. Kingsley would have us think, that it should be content to end. The notion of duty is an excellent one to start with, but it is a poor thing to spend one's life in trying to compass. A life so spent, at any rate, is not a fit subject for an epic novel. The Burtons had none but the minor virtues — honesty, energy, and a strong family feeling. Let us do all justice to these excellent qualities, but let us not shame them by for ever speaking of them with our hats off, and a "so help me God!" The only hero in Mr. Kingsley's book is, to our perception, the villain, Sir George Hillyar. *He* has a spark of inspiration; he is ridden by an evil genius; he has a spirit of his own. The others, the good persons, the gentlemen and ladies, whether developed by "a year and a half at boarding-school", or still in the rough, have nothing but the old Kingsleian *air noble*. We are informed that they have "great souls", which on small provocation rush into their eyes and into the grasp of their hands; and they are for ever addressing each other as "old boy" and "old girl." "Is *this* ambition?" Has the language of friendship and of love no finer terms than these? Those who use them, we are reminded, are gentlemen in the rough. There is, in our opinion, no such thing as a gentleman in the rough. A gentleman is born of his polish.

A great French critic characterized Mr. Carlyle in a sentence which we are confident he did not keep for what we have called the noble school of fiction, the muscular system of morals, only because its founder was unknown to him. Carlyle, said M. Taine, "would limit the human heart to the English sentiment of respect." It seems to us that these words admirably sum up Kingsleyism, the morality which Mr. Charles Kingsley preaches in his sermons, teaches in his wondrous lectures on history, and dramatizes in his novels, and of which his brother is a more worldly and popular representative. There is that in Mr. Charles Kingsley's tone which implies a conviction that when he has served up human nature in the way described by M. Taine, he has finally disposed of it. He has held up the English spirit to the imitation of the world. He has, indeed, held it up by the force of his great talents to the contemplation of a large number of spectators, and of certain admirable properties of this spirit he will long be regarded as one of the most graphic exponents. But he has shown, together with a great deal to admire, a great deal to reprove; and it is his damning fault (the expression is not too strong) that equally with its merits he would impose its defects wholesale upon the rest of mankind. But there is in the human heart a sentiment higher than that of duty — the sentiment of freedom; and in the human imagination a force which respects nothing but what is divine. In the muscular faith there is very little of the divine, because there is very little that is spiritual. For the same reason there is nothing but a spurious nobleness. Who would rest content with this as the last word of religious sagacity: that the ideal for human endeavor is the English gentleman? — unless, indeed, it be the English gentleman himself. To this do Mr. Charles Kingsley's teachings amount. There is, nevertheless, in his novels, and in his brother's as well, a great deal which we might call beautiful, if it were not that this word always suggests something that is true; a great deal which we must, therefore, be content to call pretty. Professor Kingsley would probably be by no means satisfied to have us call "Westward,

Ho!" a *pretty* story; but it *is* pretty, nevertheless; it is, in fact, quite charming. It is written in a style which the author would himself call "noble English", and it contains many lovely descriptions of South America, which he has apparently the advantage of not having visited. How a real South America would clash with his unreal England! Mr. Henry Kingsley will never do anything so good; but if he will forget a vast number of things, and remember as many more, he may write a readable story yet. Let him forget, in the first place, that he is an English gentleman, and remember that he is a novelist. Let him forget (always in the interest of art) the eternal responsibility of the rich to the poor, which in the volume before us has spoiled two good things. And let him talk a little less about nobleness, and inquire a little more closely into its real essence. We do not desire hereby to arrest the possible flights of his imagination. On the contrary, we are sure that if he will woo human nature with the proper assiduity, he will draw from her many a sweet confession, infinitely more creditable than anything he could have fancied. Only let him not consider it necessary to his success to salute her invariably as "old girl."

VII

Miss Mackenzie

WE have long entertained for Mr. Trollope a partiality of which we have yet been somewhat ashamed. Perhaps, indeed, we do wrong to say that we have entertained it. It has rather usurped our hospitality, and has resisted several attempts at forcible expulsion. If it remains, therefore, in however diminished vigor, we confess that it will be through our weakness.

Miss Mackenzie is a worthy gentlewoman, who, coming at the age of thirty-six into a comfortable little fortune, retires to enjoy it at a quiet wateringplace, where, in the course of time, she is beset by a brace of mercenary suitors. After the lapse of a year she discovers that she holds her property by a wrongful title, and is compelled to transfer it to her cousin, a widowed baronet, with several children, who, however, gallantly repairs the injury thus judicially inflicted, by making her his wife. The work may be qualified, therefore, in strictness, as the history of the pecuniary embarrassments of a middle-aged spinster. The subject has, at least, the charm of novelty, a

---

"Miss Mackenzie." By Anthony Trollope. New York: 1865.

merit of which the author has wisely appreciated the force. We had had heroines of many kinds, maidens in their teens, yea, even in their units, and matrons in their twenties, but as yet we had had no maidens in their thirties. We, for our part, have often been called upon to protest against the inveterate and excessive immaturity of the ladies in whose fortunes we are expected to interest ourselves, and we are sincerely grateful to Mr. Trollope for having practically recognized the truth that a woman is potentially a heroine as long as she lives. To many persons a middle-aged woman in love trenches upon the ridiculous. Such persons may be assured, however, that although there is considerable talk about this passion in "Miss Mackenzie", there is very little of its substance. Mr. Trollope has evidently been conscious of the precarious nature of his heroines' dignity, and in attempting to cancel the peril to which it is exposed, he has diminished the real elements of passion. This is apt to be the case in Mr. Trollope's stories. Passion has to await the convenience of so many other claimants that in the end she is but scantly served. As for action, we all know what we are to expect of Mr. Trollope in this direction; and the admirers of "quiet novels", as they are somewhat euphuistically termed, will not be disappointed here. Miss Mackenzie loses her brother, and assumes his property: she then adopts her little niece, takes lodgings at Littlebath, returns a few visits, procures a seat at church, puts her niece at school, receives a few awkward visits from a couple of vulgar bachelors, quarrels with her pastor's wife, goes to stay with some dull old relatives, loses her money, falls out with the dull relatives, is taken up by a fashionable cousin and made to serve in a fancy fair, and finally receives and accepts an offer from another cousin. Except the acquisition and loss of her property, which events are detailed at great length, she has no adventures. Her life could not well be more peaceful. She certainly suffers and enjoys less than most women. Granting, that the adventures entailed upon her by her luckless £800 a year are such as may properly mark her for our observation and compensate for the lack of incidents more dramatic, Mr. Trollope may consider that he has hit the average of the experience of unmarried English ladies. It is perhaps impossible to overstate the habitual monotony of such lives; and at all events, as far as the chronicler of domestic events has courage to go in this direction, so far will a certain proportion of facts bear him out. Literally, then, Mr. Trollope accomplishes his purpose of being true to common life. But in reading his pages, we were constantly induced to ask ourselves whether he is equally true to nature; that is, whether in the midst of this multitude of real things, of uncompromisingly real circumstances, the persons put before us are equally real. Mr. Trollope has proposed to himself to describe those facts which are so close

under every one's nose that no one notices them.
Life is vulgar, but we know not how vulgar it is
till we see it set down in his pages. It may be said,
therefore, that the emotions which depend upon
such facts as these cannot be too prosaic; that as
prison discipline makes men idiots, an approach,
however slight, to this kind of influence perceptibly
weakens the mind. We are yet compelled to
doubt whether men and women of healthy intellect take life, even in its smallest manifestation, as *stupidly* as Miss Mackenzie and her friends.
Mr. Trollope has, we conceive, simply wished to
interest us in ordinary mortals: it has not been
his intention to introduce us to a company of
imbeciles. But, seriously, we do not consider
these people to be much better. Detach them
from their circumstances, reduce them to their
essences, and what do they amount to? They are
but the halves of men and women. The accumu-
lation of minute and felicitous circumstances
which constitutes the modern novel sheds such a
glamour of reality over the figures which sustain
the action that we forbear to scrutinize them
separately. The figures are the generals in the
argument; the facts are the particulars. The
persons should accordingly reflect life upon the
details, and not borrow it from them. To do so
is only to borrow the contagion of death. This
latter part is the part they play, and with this
result, as it seems to us, in "Miss Mackenzie."
It is possible that this result is Mr. Trollope's

misfortune rather than his fault. He has encountered it in trying to avoid an error which he doubtless considers more pernicious still, that of overcharging nature. He has doubtless done his best to give us the happy middle truth. But ah, if the truth is not so black as she is sometimes painted, neither is she so pale!

We do not expect from the writers of Mr. Trollope's school (and this we esteem already a great concession) that they shall contribute to the glory of human nature; but we may at least exact that they do not wantonly detract from it. Mr. Trollope's offence is, after all, deliberate. He has deliberately selected vulgar illustrations. His choice may indeed be explained by an infirmity for which he is not responsible: we mean his lack of imagination. But when a novelist's imagination is weak, his judgment should be strong. Such was the case with Thackeray. Mr. Trollope is of course wise, in view of the infirmity in question, in devoting himself to those subjects which least expose it. He is an excellent, an admirable observer; and such an one may accomplish much. But why does he not observe great things as well as little ones? It was by doing so that Thackeray wrote "Henry Esmond." Mr. Trollope's devotion to little things, inveterate, self-sufficient as it is, begets upon the reader the very disagreeable impression that not only no imagination was required for the work before him, but that a man of imagination could not possibly have written it.

A more richly-gifted writer would miss many of his small (that is, his great) effects. It must be admitted, however, that he would obtain on the other hand a number of truly great ones. Yet, as great effects are generally produced at present by small means, Mr. Trollope is master of a wide field! He deals wholly in small effects. His manner, like most of the literary manners of the day, is a small manner. And what a strange phenomenon, when we reflect upon it, is this same small manner! What an anomaly in a work of imagination is such a chapter as that in which our author describes Mrs. Tom Mackenzie's shabby dinner party. It is as well described as it possibly could be. Nothing is omitted. It is almost as good as certain similar scenes in the "Book of Snobs." It makes the reader's ear tingle and his cheeks to redden with shame. Nothing, we say, is omitted; but, alas! nothing is infused. The scene possesses no interest but such as resides in the crude facts: and as this is null, the picture is clever, it is faithful, it is even horrible, but it is not interesting. There we touch upon the difference between the great manner and the small manner; herein lies the reason why in such scenes Mr. Trollope is only *almost* as good as Thackeray. It can generally be said of this small manner that it succeeds; cleverness is certain of success; it never has the vertigo; it is only genius and folly that fail. But in what does it succeed? That is the test question: the question which it behooves us to impose now-a-days with ever growing stringency upon works of art; for it is the answer to this question that should approve or condemn them. It is small praise to say of a novelist that he succeeds in mortifying the reader. Yet Mr. Trollope is master of but two effects: he renders his reader comfortable or the reverse. As long as he restricts himself to this scale of emotion, of course he has no need of imagination, for imagination speaks to the heart. In the scene here mentioned, Mr. Trollope, as we have said, mortifies the reader; in other scenes he fosters his equanimity, and his plan, indeed, is generally to leave him in a pleasant frame of mind.

This is all very well; and we are perhaps ill advised to expect sympathy for any harsh strictures upon a writer who renders such excellent service. Let us, however, plainly disavow a harsh intention. Let us, in the interest of our argument, heartily recognize his merits. His merits, indeed! he has only too many. His manner is literally freckled with virtues. We use this term advisedly, because its virtues are all virtues of detail: the virtues of the photograph. The photograph lacks the supreme virtue of possessing a character. It is the detail alone that distinguishes one photograph from another. What but the details distinguishes one of Mr. Trollope's novels from another, and, if we may use the expression, consigns it to itself? Of course the details are charming, some of them ineffably charming. The

ingenuous loves, the innocent flirtations, of Young
England, have been described by Mr. Trollope
in such a way as to secure him the universal
public good-will; described minutely, sympatheti-
.cally, accurately; if it were not that an indefinable
instinct bade us to keep the word in reserve, we
should say truthfully. The story of Miss Mackenzie lacks this element of vernal love-making.
The most that can be said of the affairs of this
lady's heart is that they are not ridiculous. They
are assuredly not interesting; and they are involved in much that is absolutely repulsive.
When you draw on the grand scale, a certain
amount of coarseness in your lines is excusable;
but when you work with such short and cautious
strokes as Mr. Trollope, it behooves you, above
all things, to be delicate. Still, taking the book in
its best points, the development of Miss Mackenzie's affections would not, in actual life, be a
phenomenon worthy of an intelligent spectator.
What rights, then, accrue to it in print? Miss
Mackenzie is an utterly commonplace person,
and her lover is almost a fool. He is apparently
unsusceptible of the smallest inspiration from the
events of his life. Why should we follow the fortunes of such people? They vulgarize experience
and all the other heavenly gifts. Why should we
stop to gather nettles when there are roses bloom-
ing under our hands? Why should we batten upon
over-cooked prose while the air is redolent with
undistilled poetry? It is perhaps well that we

should learn how superficial, how spiritless, how literal human feeling may become; but is a novel here our proper lesson-book? Clever novels may be manufactured of such material as this; but to outweigh a thousand merits they will have the one defect, that they are *monstrous*. They will be anomalies. Mr. Matthew Arnold, however, has recently told us that a large class of Englishmen consider it no objection to a thing that it is an anomaly. Mr. Trollope is doubtless one of the number.

VIII

The Schönberg-Cotta Family

THE wide circulation obtained by this work and its successors we attribute to their clever interfusion, and, indeed, we might almost say confusion, of history and fiction with religion. They offer neither the best history, the best piety, nor the best fiction, but they appeal to a public which has long since become reconciled to compromise — that extensive public, so respectable in everything but its literary taste, which patronizes what is called "Sunday reading." We do not propose to examine the theory of this branch of literature. It is an implicitly accepted fact. We propose simply to offer a few remarks upon the works before us as its fruit.

The foremost property of the school to which these works belong is an attempted, and, to a certain degree, successful compromise between the interests of youth and those of maturity, between the serious and the trivial. This, indeed,

---

"Hearthstone Series: Chronicles of the Schönberg-Cotta Family; The Early Dawn: Sketches of Christian Life in England in the Olden Time; Sketches of the United Brethren of Bohemia and Moravia; Diary of Mrs. Kitty Trevylyan: a Story of the Times of Whitefield and the Wesleys." New York: 1865.

is the mark of a vast proportion of the efforts of modern book-making — efforts which in their aggregate may be regarded as an attempt to provide a special literature for women and children, to provide books which grown women may read aloud to children without either party being bored. Books of this class never aim at anything so simple as merely to entertain. They frequently contain, as in the present case, an infusion of religious and historical information, and they in all cases embody a moral lesson. This latter fact is held to render them incompetent as novels; and doubtless, after all, it does, for of a genuine novel the meaning and the lesson are infinite; and here they are carefully narrowed down to a special precept.

It would be unjust to deny that these semi-developed novels are often very charming. Occasionally, like the "Heir of Redclyffe", they almost legitimate themselves by the force of genius. But this only when a first-rate mind takes the matter in hand. By a first-rate mind we here mean a mind which (since its action is restricted beforehand to the shortest gait, the smallest manners possible this side of the ridiculous) is the master and not the slave of its material. It is just now very much the fashion to discuss the so-called principle of realism, and we all know that there exists in France a school of art in which it is associated with great brilliancy and great immorality. The disciples of this school pursue, with an assiduity worthy of a better cause, the research of local colors, with which they have produced a number of curious effects. We believe, however, that the greatest successes in this line are reserved for that branch of the school which contains the most female writers; for if women are unable to draw, they notoriously can at all events paint, and this is what realism requires. For an exhibition of the true realistic *chic* we would accordingly refer that body of artists who are represented in France by MM. Flaubert and Gérome to that class of works which in our literature are represented by the "Daisy Chain" and "The Wide, Wide World", and to which the "Chronicles" before us essentially belong. Until the value of *chic* can be finally established, we should doubtless be thankful that in our literature it lends its vivifying force only to objects and sensations of the most unquestioned propriety. In these "Chronicles," for instance, it is impressed into the service of religion. In this particular instance, the healthy, if not very lively, fancy of the author, her pleasant style, and her apparent religious sincerity, secure a result which on the whole is not uninteresting. But the radical defects of the theological novel come out strongly in the "Diary of Mrs. Kitty Trevylyan", where the story is but a thin coating for a bitter pill of Methodism. We are all of us Protestants, and we are all of us glad to see the Reformation placed in its most favorable light, but as we are not all of us Methodists, it is hard to sympathize with a lady's *ex parte* treatment of John Wesley. Our authoress does not claim to be more than superficial, and it were better not to touch Methodism at all than to handle it superficially. It is probably impossible that such of the phenomena of Methodism as might with any show of likelihood find an echo in the daily jottings of an ordinary country girl should be other than repulsive to the impartial reader.

The "Chronicles" present a kind of tabular view of the domestic pursuits of a group of growing boys and girls, contemporaries and friends of Martin Luther. Of this, the central figure in her narrative, the authoress has discreetly given us only a portrait in profile. Her object has been to give us a household picture of the Reformation. But it is the misfortune of short-gaited writers that they are unable to carry out an idea which demands any continuity of purpose. They enjoy, however, this compensation, that if they do not succeed in one thing, they may reasonably be held to have succeeded in another. Of history in the "Chronicles" there is just as much as may have been obtained by an attentive perusal of M. Merle d'Aubigné. But there is a great deal of what has been very wittily called "*her* story." A very small part of the Reformation must necessarily have been seen from the leaded window-panes of an obscure Saxon printer. But a certain infinitesimal portion of it may very naturally have transpired in the quaint and wainscotted rooms behind these window-panes, especially if the printer's family happened to boast the acquaintance of Doctor Luther. When we have said that the author has conveyed the impression of all this Gothic furniture with tolerable success, we have given to the truthfulness of her work the highest praise at our command. For this a pleasing fancy was alone required; but for those more difficult portions which involved the reconstruction of feelings and ideas, there was need of that vigorous imagination and that serious reflection which can stand on tiptoe and overlook three centuries of civilization.

The author's whole tone is the tone of the retrospective present. She anticipates throughout the judgments of posterity. Morally, her young chroniclers are of the nineteenth century, or they at least have had access to it. The subjects of great revolutions are like the rank and file of great armies, they are all unconscious of the direction and force of the movement to which they contribute. Our civil war has taught us, among so many other valuable lessons, the gross natural blindness — that is, we are bound in reason to believe, the clear spiritual insight — of great popular impulses. It has intimated that if these were of men only they would often miscarry for very shame. But men's natural deserts are frequently at variance with their spiritual needs; and they are allowed to execute the divine plan not only by their own petty practices, but on their own petty theories; not only by obedience but by spontaneity. We are very apt to do small things in God's name, but God does great things in ours. The sagacious Schönbergs-Cotta are by far too divinely illumined, too well aware of what they want, and of what they are likely to get. There must have been a great deal more of feeling than of thought in the Reformation, and almost as much of action as of either. People loved and hated, and feared and fought, and — a fact, we imagine, which is near the bottom of much that is of revolutionary effect — were dreadfully nervous; but we may be certain that they did not moralize as we moralize now-a-days. Protestantism is still on the whole sufficiently orthodox; but we are all of us more or less Unitarians in spirit compared with the founders of our creed. What was done both by them and by their opponents was done in the absolute name of religion. How then should it have been done at all? "When half-gods go," says Emerson, "the gods arrive." Assuredly, when the gods arrive, the half-gods depart. When religion enters in force, moral pre-occupations withdraw. Duty was not probably an habitual topic with the Reformers. We doubt whether a simple burgher's daughter was familiar with the word "conscientious." That she had a conscience is eminently probable, but we hardly believe that she knew it. Nor can we conceive her to have been troubled with "views" or "difficulties." But however this may be, let us not bear severely on any honest attempt to revive the great facts of the past. If people must indulge in the composition of ingenious nothings, let their nothings be about a central something. Let us hang our fancies rather upon the immortal than upon the ephemeral. Works like the present affect the great figure of history as much and as little as the travelling cloud-shadows affect the insensitive mountains.

IX

Can You Forgive Her?

THIS new novel of Mr. Trollope's has nothing new to teach us either about Mr. Trollope himself as a novelist, about English society as a theme for the novelist, or, failing information on these points, about the complex human heart. Take any one of his former tales, change the names of half the characters, leave the others standing, and transpose the incidents, and you will have "Can You Forgive Her?" It is neither better nor worse than the tale which you will select. It became long ago apparent that Mr. Trollope had only one manner. In this manner he very soon showed us his *maximum*. He has recently, in "Miss Mackenzie", showed us his *minimum*. In the work before us he has remained pretty constantly at his best. There is, indeed, a certain amount of that inconceivably vulgar love-making between middle-aged persons by which "Miss Mackenzie" was distinguished; but the burden of the story rests upon the young people.

For so thick a book, there is certainly very little story. There are no less than three different plots,

"Can You Forgive Her?" By Anthony Trollope. New York: 1865.

however, if the word can be applied to Mr. Trollope's simple machinations. That is, there is a leading story, which, being foreseen at the outset to be insufficient to protract the book during the requisite number of months, is padded with a couple of underplots, one of which comes almost near being pathetic, as the other falls very far short of being humorous. The main narrative, of course, concerns the settlement in life — it is hard to give it a more sentimental name — of a beautiful young lady. Alice Vavasar, well-born, high-spirited, motherless, and engaged to Mr. John Grey, the consummate model of a Christian gentleman, mistrusting the quality of her affection, breaks off her engagement, after which, in a moment of enthusiasm, she renews an anterior engagement with her cousin, George Vavasar, a plausible rascal. John Grey will not be put off, however, and steadfastly maintains his suit. In the course of time George's villany is discovered. He attempts, unsuccessfully, to murder Grey. Grey follows his mistress, pleads his cause once more, and is taken back again. The question is, Can we forgive Miss Vavasar? Of course we can, and forget her, too, for that matter. What does Mr. Trollope mean by this question? It is a good instance of the superficial character of his work that he has been asking it once a month for so long a time without being struck by its flagrant impertinence. What are we to forgive? Alice Vavasar's ultimate acceptance of John Grey

makes her temporary ill-treatment of him, viewed
as a moral question, a subject for mere drawing-
room gossip. There are few of Mr. Trollope's
readers who will not resent being summoned to
pass judgment on such a sin as the one here presented, to establish by precedent the criminality
of the conscientious flutterings of an excellent
young lady. Charming women, thanks to the
talent of their biographers, have been forgiven
much greater improprieties. Since forgiveness
was to be brought into the question, why did not
Mr. Trollope show us an error that we might
really forgive — an error that would move us to
indignation? It is too much to be called upon to
take cognizance in novels of sins against conven-
tion, of improprieties; we have enough of these in
life. We can have charity and pity only for real
sin and real misery. We trust to novels to maintain us in the practice of great indignations and
great generosities. Miss Vavasar's dilemma is
doubtless considerable enough in itself, but by
the time it is completely unfolded by Mr. Trollope
it has become so trivial, it is associated with so
much that is of a merely accidental interest, it is
so deflowered of the bloom of a serious experience,
that when we are asked to enter into it judicially,
we feel almost tempted to say that really it is
Miss Vavasar's own exclusive business. From the
moment that a novel comes to a happy conclusion, we can forgive everything — or nothing.
The gradual publication of "Can You Forgive

Her?" made its readers familiar with the appeal resting upon their judgment long before they were in a position to judge. The only way, it seems to us, to justify this appeal and to obviate the flagrant anti-climax which the work now presents, was to lead the story to a catastrophe, to leave the heroine *prima facie* in the wrong, to make her rupture with Grey, in a word, final. Then we might have forgiven her in consideration of the lonely years of repentance in store for her, and of her having been at any rate consistent. Then the world's forgiveness would have been of some importance to her. Now, at one for ever with her lover, what matters our opinion? It certainly matters very little to ourselves.

Mr. Trollope's book presents no feature more remarkable than the inveteracy with which he just eludes being really serious; unless it be the almost equal success with which he frequently escapes being really humorous. Both of these results are the penalty of writing so rapidly; but as in much rapid writing we are often made to regret the absence of that sober second thought which may curtail an extravagance — that critical movement which, if you will only give it time, is surely to follow the creative one — so in Mr. Trollope we perpetually miss that sustained action of the imagination, that creative movement which in those in whom this faculty is not supreme *may*, if you will give it time, bear out the natural or critical one, which would intensify and animate his first conception. We are for ever wishing that he would go a little further, a little deeper. There are a hundred places in "Can You Forgive Her?" where even the dullest readers will be sure to express this wish. For ourselves, we were very much disappointed that when Alice returns to her cousin George she should not do so more frankly, that on eventually restoring herself to Grey she should have so little to expiate or to forget, that she should leave herself, in short, so easy an issue by her refusal to admit Vavasar to a lover's privilege. Our desire for a different course of action is simply founded on the fact that it would have been so much more interesting. When it is proposed to represent a young girl as jilting her lover in such a way as that the moral of the tale resolves itself into the question of the venality of her offence, it evinces in the novelist a deep insensibility to his opportunities that he should succeed, after all, in making of the tragedy but a simple postponement of the wedding-day.

To Mr. Trollope all the possible incidents of society seem to be of equal importance and of equal interest. He has the same treatment, the same tone, for them all. After narrating the minutest particulars of a certain phase of his heroine's experience, he will dwell with equal length and great patience upon the proceedings of a vulgar widow (the heroine's aunt), who is engaged in playing fast and loose with a couple of vulgar suitors. With what authority can we

invest the pen which treats of the lovely niece,
when we see it devoted with the same good-will
to the utterly prosaic and unlovely aunt? It is
of course evident that Mr. Trollope has not intended to make the aunt either poetic or attrac-
tive. He has intended, in the first place, to swell
his book into the prescribed dimensions, and, incidentally, to make the inserted matter amusing.
A single chapter of it might be amusing; a dozen
chapters are inexpressibly wearisome. The undue prominence assigned to this episode is yet
not so signal an offence against good judgment as
the subordination of Lady Glencora Palliser's
story to that of Alice Vavasar's. It is a great
mistake in speaking of a novel to be over-positive
as to what ought to be and what ought not; but
we do not fear to dogmatize when we say that by
rights Lady Glencora is the heroine of the book.
Her adventure is more important, more dramatic,
more interesting than Alice Vavasar's. That it is
more interesting is not a matter of opinion, but a
matter of fact. A woman who forsakes her husband belongs more to the technical heroic than a
woman who merely forsakes her lover. Lady
Glencora, young and fascinating, torn from the
man of her heart and married to a stranger, and
pursued after marriage by her old lover, handsome, dissolute, desperate, touches at a hundred
points almost upon the tragical. And yet her history gets itself told as best it may, in the intervals
of what is after all, considering the *dénouement*,

but a serious comedy. It is, to use a common illustration, as if Mr. Forest should appear on the "off-nights" of no matter what fainter dramatic luminary. It signifies little in the argument that Lady Glencora's adventure came also to an anticlimax; for in this case the reader rejects the conclusion as a mere begging of the issue. Of all literary sinners Mr. Trollope deserves fewest hard words, but we can scarcely refrain from calling this conclusion impudent. To a real novelist's eye, the story on which it depends is hardly begun; to Mr. Trollope, it is satisfactorily ended. The only explanation of all this is probably that the measure of his invention is not in his subject, in his understanding with his own mind; but outside of it, in his understanding with his publishers. Poor little Lady Glencora, with her prettiness, her grace, her colossal fortune, and her sorrows, is the one really poetic figure in the novel. Why not have dealt her a little poetic justice? Why not, for *her* sake, have shown a little boldness? We do not presume to prescribe to Mr. Trollope the particular thing he should have done; we simply affirm in general terms that he should have gone further. Everything forbade that Lady Glencora and her lover should be vulgarly disposed of. What are we to conclude? It is easy to conceive either that Burgo Fitzgerald slowly wasted his life, or that he flung it suddenly away. But the supposition is by no means easy that Lady Glencora either wasted hers or carefully

BY HENRY JAMES

economized it. Besides, there is no pretence of
winding up Burgo Fitzgerald's thread; it is rudely
clipped by the editorial shears. There is, on the
contrary, a pretence of completing the destiny of
his companion. But we have more respect for
Lady Glencora's humanity than to suppose that
the incident on which the curtain of her little
tragedy falls, is for her anything more than an
interruption. Another case in which Mr. Trollope had burdened himself, as he proceeded, with
the obligation to go further, is that of George
Vavasar. Upon him, as upon Lady Glencora,
there hangs a faint reflection of poetry. In both
these cases, Mr. Trollope, dealing with an un-
familiar substance, seems to have evoked a ghost
which he cannot exorcise. As the reader follows
George Vavasar deeper into his troubles — all of
which are very well described — his excited imagination hankers for — what shall we say? Nothing less positive than Vavasar's death. Here was
a chance for Mr. Trollope to redeem a thousand
pages of small talk; the wretched man should have
killed himself; for although bloodshed is not quite
so common an element of modern life as the sensation writers would have us believe, yet people
do occasionally, when hard pushed, commit suicide. But for Mr. Trollope anything is preferable to a sensation; an incident is ever preferable
to an event. George Vavasar simply takes ship
to America.

X

The Gayworthys

THIS book appears to have been suggested by a fanciful theory of life, which the author embodies in a somewhat over-figurative preface, and which recurs throughout the story at intervals, like a species of refrain. The theory in question amounts to neither more nor less than this: that life is largely made up of broken threads, of plans arrested in their development, of hopes untimely crushed. This idea is neither very new nor very profound; but the novel formula under which it is shadowed forth on the title-page will probably cause it to strike many well-disposed minds as for the first time. In a story written in the interest of a theory two excellent things are almost certain to be spoiled. It might seem, indeed, that it would be a very small figure of a story that could be injured by a theory like the present one; but when once an author has his dogma at heart, unless he is very much of an artist, it is sure to become obtrusive at the capital moment, and to remind the reader that he is, after all, learning a moral lesson. The slightly ingenious and very superficial figure in which the author

---

"The Gayworthys: a Story of Threads and Thrums." [By Mrs. A. D. T. Whitney.] Boston: 1865.

embodies her philosophy recurs with a frequency which is truly impertinent.

Our story is organized upon three main threads, which, considering the apparent force of the author's conviction, are on the whole very tenderly handled; inasmuch as, although two of them are at moments drawn so tight that we are fully prepared for the final snap and the quiet triumph of the author's "I told you so," yet only one of them is really severed past all repair. This catastrophe symbolizes the fate of Miss Rebecca Gayworthy, who cherishes a secret flame for her pastor, the Rev. Jordan King. Mr. King, in turn, entertains a passion for another young lady, whom he marries, but who is not all for him that Miss Gayworthy would have been. The broken thread here is Miss Gayworthy's slighted regard for Mr. King.

There are two other pairs of lovers whose much shifting relations fill up the rest of the book. Miss Joanna Gayworthy is gifted, for her misfortune, with a lively tongue and an impetuous temper. She is kept for a number of years the subject of one of those gratuitous misconceptions in which lady novelists delight. To our mind there is quite as much of the comical as of the pathetic in her misunderstanding with Gabriel Hartshorne. Both she and her lover seem bent on fixing the *minimum* of words with which a courtship can be conducted, and the utmost possible impertinence of those words. They fall the natural victims to their own ingenuity. The fault, however, is more with him than with her. If she was a little too much of a coquette, he was far too little of an enthusiast. Women have a prescriptive right to answer indirectly at serious moments; but men labor under a prescriptive obligation at these moments to speak and act to the point. We cannot but think that Gabriel obtained his mistress quite as soon as he had won her.

Of the parties yet mentioned, however, neither is to be taken for the hero and heroine proper; for in the presence of the inevitable, the orthodox little girl, — this time, fortunately, matched not with a condescending man of the world, but with a lad of her own age, — in the presence, we say, of these heroic figures, who shall dare to claim that distinction? Sarah Gair and Gershom Vorse are brought up together in the fields, like another Daphnis and Chloe. Gershom is sent to sea by the machinations of Sarah's mother, who has a quasi-prophetic insight into what may be. Sarah blossoms into young ladyhood, and Gershom obtains command of a vessel. In the course of time he comes home, but, we regret to say, with little of the breezy gallantry of his profession. For long years his old playmate has worn his image upon her heart of hearts. He utterly fails to take cognizance of her attachment, and in fact snubs her most unmercifully. Thrums again, as you see. It is perhaps hard to overstate the possibilities of man's insensibility as opposed to woman's cunning devotion. But the whole picture of Gershom Vorse strikes us as ill-conceived; and yet those who remember Tom Tulliver in "The Mill on the Floss" will acknowledge that much can be made in a dramatic way of the figure of the rational, practical, honest, prejudiced youth whose responsibilities begin early. It is perhaps natural that Gershom Vorse's contempt for the mother should have predisposed him against the daughter; but why should he nurse so unmannerly an intolerance of all her little woman's graces? If Sarah was really a perfect young lady, she was too good for this grim and precocious Puritan. He despises her because, being a young lady, she looks and dresses like one, because she wears "puffed muslin and dainty boots." Out upon him! What should he care about such things? That this trait is not manly, we need not affirm; but it is the reverse of masculine.

It is hardly worth while, however, to criticise details in an episode which is so radically defective as this one. Its radical defect is the degradation of sentiment by making children responsible for it. This practice is becoming the bane of our novels. It signifies little where it began, or what authority it claims: it is, in our opinion, as fatal to the dignity of serious feeling and to the grandeur of strong passions as the most flagrant immoralities of French fiction. Heaven defend us from the puerile! If we desire to read about children, we shall not be at loss: the repertory of juvenile works is vast. But if we desire to learn the various circumstances under which love-making may be conducted, let us not repair to the nursery and the school-room. A man's childhood and his manhood can never, without a violation of truth, be made the same story; much less may the youth and maturity of a woman. In "The Gayworthys" the loves of the two young people are far too exclusively projected from their infancy. The age for Daphnis and Chloe has passed. Passion and sentiment must always be more or less intelligent not to shock the public taste. There are, of course, few things so charming as the innocence of childhood, just as there are few things so interesting as the experience of manhood. But they cannot in a love-story be successfully combined. Thackeray's great genius was insufficient to prevent the fruition of Henry Esmond's boyish devotion from seeming very disagreeable. Every reader feels that, if he had had the story to write, *that* should not have been its consummation. There is in the experience of every man and woman a certain proportion of sensations which are interesting only to themselves. To this class of feelings we would refer the childish reminiscences held in common by two persons who at the age of discretion unite their destinies. A man seldom falls in love with the young girl who has grown up at his side; he either likes or dislikes her too much. But when he does, it is from quite a new stand-point and with a new range of feelings. He does not woo her in the name of their juvenile *escapades*. These are pretty only in after years, when there is no other poetry to be had. And they are, therefore, quite apart from the purposes of the serious novelist.

So much for the faults of "The Gayworthys." Let us now pay the tribute of an explicit recognition to its very great cleverness. Without this quality no novel in these days can hope to succeed. But "The Gayworthys" has even more of it than is needed for success. How many accomplishments the would-be successful novel demands! and how many are here displayed! When we count them over, indeed, we are half amazed at our temerity in offering these prosy strictures. The observation, the memory, the invention, the fancy, the humor, the love of human nature, lavished upon these four hundred pages are the results almost of an education. Let us, we repeat, make them a very low bow. They contain much that is admirable and much that is powerful. It is for this reason that, when we see them misused, as it seems to us, conjoined with what is vulgar and false, we make a respectful protest. We know not whether in this case their union makes a total which we may properly call genius; but it at all events makes a force sufficiently like genius not to be able with impunity to work in ignorance of principle. We do not claim to have laid down any principles. They are already laid down in a thousand consummate works of art. All we wish to do here — all we have space to do — is to remind the author of "The Gayworthys" that they exist.

XI

A French Critic

TO the first series of these literary studies, published two years ago, M. Scherer attached a preface which he doubtless intends shall serve also for this second volume. A short glance at this preface will initiate us into the author's view of the limits of his own work. "Custom exacts", says M. Scherer, "that a preface should sum up the doctrines of the book. But suppose the book has no doctrines? I find many subjects handled in these pages: philosophy, religion, literature, history, politics, morals — there is a little of all these. If, indeed, I start no ideas on these subjects, I speak of men who have done so. But in the midst of all this I look in vain for the least sign of a doctrine. Nay, what is worse, the book seems to me to be full of inconsistencies, or, as some might say, of contradictions. I find myself to-day all latitude, and to-morrow all indignation; now a rigid moralist, now a disinterested critic; now tolerant as a philosopher, now strenuous as a partizan." To the critic duly reproached with these inconsistencies, pursues M. Scherer, there

---

"Nouvelles Études sur la Littérature Contemporaine." By Edmond Scherer. Paris: 1865.

remains this resource: to accept the reproach, and to reduce it to its proper value. This M. Scherer proceeds to do in his own case. At bottom, he affirms, rightly understood, no serious mind ever contradicts itself. To accuse a man of so doing is simply to display covertly your own ignorance. How can we know those secret reasons, those blind instincts, those confused motives, which the subject of them himself only half suspects? We think that a man has changed when he has only pursued or achieved his natural manifestation. There are in the tyranny of circumstances and the inherent inflexibility of ideas a hundred obstacles to the complete expression of feelings. These feelings, which constitute a man's real substance, his inclinations, his affections, his aspirations, never change. The nearest approach they make to it is to develop by a strictly logical process. In default of doctrines in a work — or, as we should say, in default of a system, of a consistent argument — there is always, accordingly, a certain irrepressible moral substance. This moral substance in his own work M. Scherer declares to be the love of liberty. He loves liberty as the necessary condition of truth, of thorough examination, of impartiality. "Contention, written and spoken", says M. Scherer, "the opposition and the fusion of opinions, errors, retractions, excuses, reactions: all these things are the formation of truth." And these things are only possible under liberty. "Truth", he con-

tinues, "is for me simply improvement; and liberty is scarcely more than another name for this
constant process of improvement."

M. Scherer's merits, then, as a critic, are these:
that he has no doctrines, and that in default of
these he is prompted by as excellent a feeling as
the love of liberty. It may seem questionable at
first whether the former fact is really a merit. It
is not that in reading M. Scherer's volume we
do not find much that is positive: many opinions,
much sympathy, much dissent, much philosophy,
much strong feeling; for without these the reproach of inconsistency would be impossible. We
find much that we can specifically approve or
condemn. We find even plenty of theories. But
this touches perhaps the very point. There are
plenty of theories, but no theory. We find — and
this is the highest praise, it seems to us, that we
can give a critic — none but a moral unity: that
is, the author is a liberal. It is hard to say, in
reading M. Scherer's books, which is the most
pleasing phenomenon, this intellectual eclecticism
or this moral consistency. The age surely presents no finer spectacle than that of a mind liberal
after this fashion; not from a brutal impatience of
order, but from experience, from reflection, seriously, intelligently, having known, relished, and
appropriated the many virtues of conservatism;
a mind inquisitive of truth and of knowledge,
accessible on all sides, unprejudiced, desirous
above all things to examine directly, fearless of

reputed errors, but merciless to error when proved, tolerant of dissent, respectful of sincerity, content neither to reason on matters of feeling nor to sentimentalize on matters of reason, equitable, dispassionate, sympathetic. M. Scherer is a solid embodiment of Mr. Matthew Arnold's ideal critic. Those who affirmed Mr. Arnold's ideal to be impracticable may here be refuted; those who thought it undesirable may perhaps be converted. For they will see that once granted M. Scherer's seriousness, his competency to the treatment of a given subject rests entirely upon his intellectual independence or irresponsibility. Of all men who deal with ideas, the critic is essentially the least independent; it behooves him, therefore, to claim the utmost possible incidental or extrinsic freedom. His subject and his stand-point are limited beforehand. He is in the nature of his function *opposed* to his author, and his position, therefore, depends upon that which his author has taken. If, in addition to his natural and proper servitude to his subject, he is shackled with a further servitude, outside of his subject, he works at a ridiculous disadvantage. This outer servitude may either be to a principle, a theory, a doctrine, a dogma, or it may be to a party; and it is against this latter form of subordination, as most frequent in his own country, that Mr. Arnold more especially protests. But as a critic, quite as much as any other writer, must have what M. Scherer calls an inspiration of his own, must possess a *unit* of sincerity and consistency, he finds it in his conscience. It is on this basis that he preserves his individuality, or, if you like, his self-respect. It is from this moral sense, and, we may add, from their religious convictions, that writers like Scherer derive that steadfast and delicate spiritual force which animates, co-ordinates, and harmonizes the mass of brief opinions, of undeveloped assertions, of conjectures, of fancies, of sentiments, which are the substance of this work.

There are, of course, degrees in criticism as in everything else. There is small criticism and there is great criticism. But great criticism seems to us to touch more or less nearly on pure philosophy. Pure criticism must be of the small kind. Goethe is a great critic; M. Sainte-Beuve is a small one. Goethe has laid down general principles. M. Sainte-Beuve has laid down particular principles; and, above all, he has observed facts and stated results. Goethe frequently starts from an idea; M. Sainte-Beuve starts from a fact: Goethe from a general rule, M. Sainte-Beuve from a particular instance. When we reflect upon all the faculties and all the accomplishments needed by the literary critic in these days, we are almost tempted to say that he should unite in himself the qualities which are required for success in every other department of letters. But we may more strictly sum up his necessary character by saying that he is a compromise between the philosopher and the historian. We spoke of M. Sainte-Beuve, who, on the whole, may be called the first of living critics. He is a philosopher in so far as that he deals with ideas. He counts, weighs, measures, appraises them. But he is not a philosopher in so far as that he works with no supreme object. There results from his work no deliberate theory of life, of nature, of the universe. He is not, as the philosopher must ever be more or less, a partizan. When he pulls down, it lies in his discretion or his generosity to build up again; whereas the philosopher is for ever offering the better in exchange for the worse — that which is more true in exchange for that which is less. The philosopher's function is to compare a work with an abstract principle of truth; the critic's is to compare a work with itself, with its own concrete standard of truth. The critic deals, therefore, with parts, the philosopher with wholes. In M. Sainte-Beuve, however, it is the historian who is most generously represented. As a critic, he bears the same relation to facts that he does to ideas. As the metaphysician handles ideas with a preconceived theory, so the historian handles facts with a preconcerted plan. But with this theory or this plan, the critic has nothing to do. He works on the small scale, in detail, looking neither before him, behind him, nor on either side. Like Mr. Ruskin's model young painter with his landscape, M. Sainte-Beuve covers up all history but the small square field under his eye. On this field, however, he works with pre-Raphaelite minuteness; he exhausts it. Then he shifts his window-frame, as we may call it, and begins again. The essence of the practicability of history is in a constant obedience to proportion. M. Sainte-Beuve, like a true critic, ignores proportion. The reunion of his chapters, therefore, would make no history, any more than the reunion of the young pre-Raphaelite's studies would make a picture.

M. Scherer's place among the critics of the time is very high. If M. Sainte-Beuve has earned the highest place, M. Scherer has a claim to the next. For ourselves, we prefer M. Scherer. He has not M. Sainte-Beuve's unrivalled power of reproducing the physiognomy of a particular moment as of a particular figure of the past; he cannot pick out some obscure secondary figure of the seventeenth century — some forgotten *littérateur*, some momentary king's mistress — and in twenty pages place the person before you as a complete human being, to be for ever remembered, with a distinct personality, with a character, an expression, a face, a dress, habits, eccentricities. M. Scherer, we say, has not done this. But we prefer him because his morality is positive without being obtrusive; and because, besides the distinction of beauty and ugliness, the æsthetic distinction of right and wrong, there constantly occurs in his pages the moral distinction between good and evil; because, in short, we salute in this fact that wisdom which, after having made the journey round the whole sphere of knowledge, returns at last with a melancholy joy to morality.

If we have a complaint, indeed, to make of M. Sainte-Beuve, it is that with all his experience he is not more melancholy. On great subjects, subjects of the first order, M. Scherer is as efficient as the author of the "Causeries de Lundi." He has judged his contemporaries quite as keenly: witness his article on M. Veuillot. And in the volume under notice are two papers, one on Mme. de Sévigné, the other on Mme. Roland, which are delicate with all M. Sainte-Beuve's delicacy, and eloquent with more than his eloquence. If we were tempted to set another critic before M. Scherer, that critic would be M. Taine. But on reflection we conclude that M. Taine is not pre-eminently a critic. He is alternately a philosopher and a historian. His strong point is not to discriminate shades of difference. On the contrary, he is perpetually sacrificing shades to broad lines. He is valuable for his general views, his broad retrospects, his *résumés*. He passes indeed, incidentally, very shrewd literary judgments, as when, for instance, he says of Swift's poetry that instead of creating illusions it destroys them. But he is too passionate, too partial, too eloquent. The critic is useful in repairing the inevitable small injustices committed by other writers; in going over the ground after them and restoring the perverted balance of truth. Now in Taine's "History of English Literature", which is nominally a critical work, there is in each chapter abundant room for this supplementary process of the critic proper. In the work of M. Scherer there is room but for contradiction — which is, in fact, a forcible making of room. With him, analysis has reached its furthest limits, and it is because he is more analytic than Mr. Taine — admitting, as we do, that he has not his genius — that we place him higher as a critic. Of M. Scherer's religious character we have not explicitly spoken, because we cannot speak of it properly in these limits. We can only say that in religion, as in everything else, he is a liberal; and we can pay no higher tribute to his critical worth than by adding that he has found means to unite the keenest theological penetration and the widest theological erudition with the greatest spiritual tolerance.

XII

Miss Braddon

MISS AURORA FLOYD, as half the world knows, was a young lady who got into no end of trouble by marrying her father's groom. We had supposed that this adventure had long ago become an old story; but here is a new edition of her memoirs to prove that the public has not done with her yet. We would assure those individuals who look with regret upon this assumption by a "sensation" novel of the honors of legitimate fiction, that the author of "Aurora Floyd" is an uncommonly clever person. Her works are distinguished by a quality for which we can find no better name than "pluck"; and should not pluck have its reward wherever found? If common report is correct, Miss Braddon had for many years beguiled the leisure moments of an arduous profession — the dramatic profession — by the composition of fictitious narrative. But until the publication of "Lady Audley's Secret" she failed to make her mark. To what secret impulse or inspiration we owe this sudden reversal of fortune it is difficult to say; but the grim de-

"Aurora Floyd." By M. E. Braddon. New York : 1865.

termination to succeed is so apparent in every line of "Lady Audley's Secret", that the critic is warranted in conjecturing that she had at last become desperate. People talk of novels with a purpose; and from this class of works, both by her patrons and her enemies, Miss Braddon's tales are excluded. But what novel ever betrayed a more resolute purpose than the production of what we may call Miss Braddon's second manner? Her purpose was at any hazard to make a hit, to catch the public ear. It was a difficult task, but audacity could accomplish it. Miss Braddon accordingly resorted to extreme measures, and created the sensation novel. It is to this audacity, this courage of despair, as manifested in her later works, that we have given the name of pluck. In these works it has settled down into a quiet determination not to let her public get ahead of her. A writer who has suddenly leaped into a popularity greatly disproportionate to his merit, can only retain his popularity by observing a strictly respectful attitude to his readers. This has been Miss Braddon's attitude, and she has maintained it with unwearied patience. She has been in her way a disciple as well as a teacher. She has kept up with the subtle innovations to which her art, like all others, is subject, as well as with the equally delicate fluctuations of the public taste. The result has been a very obvious improvement in her style.

She had been preceded in the same path by

Mr. Wilkie Collins, whose "Woman in White",
with its diaries and letters and its general ponder-
osity, was a kind of nineteenth century version of
"Clarissa Harlowe." Mind, we say a nineteenth
century version. To Mr. Collins belongs the
credit of having introduced into fiction those most
mysterious of mysteries, the mysteries which are
at our own doors. This innovation gave a new
impetus to the literature of horrors. It was fatal
to the authority of Mrs. Radcliffe and her ever-
lasting castle in the Apennines. What are the
Apennines to us, or we to the Apennines? Instead
of the terrors of "Udolpho", we were treated to
the terrors of the cheerful country-house and the
busy London lodgings. And there is no doubt
that these were infinitely the more terrible. Mrs.
Radcliffe's mysteries were romances pure and
simple; while those of Mr. Wilkie Collins were
stern reality. The supernatural, which Mrs. Radcliffe constantly implies, though she generally
saves her conscience, at the eleventh hour, by ex-
plaining it away, requires a powerful imagination
in order to be as exciting as the natural, as Mr.
Collins and Miss Braddon, without any imagination at all, know how to manage it. A good
ghost-story, to be half as terrible as a good mur-
der-story, must be connected at a hundred points
with the common objects of life. The best ghost-
story probably ever written — a tale published
some years ago in *Blackwood's Magazine* — was
constructed with an admirable understanding of

this principle. Half of its force was derived from its prosaic, commonplace, daylight accessories. Less delicately terrible, perhaps, than the vagaries of departed spirits, but to the full as *interesting*, as the modern novel reader understands the word, are the numberless possible forms of human malignity. Crime, indeed, has always been a theme for dramatic poets; but with the old poets its dramatic interest lay in the fact that it compromised the criminal's moral repose. Whence else is the interest of *Orestes* and *Macbeth?* With Mr. Collins and Miss Braddon (our modern Euripides and Shakespeare) the interest of crime is in the fact that it compromises the criminal's personal safety. The play is a tragedy, not in virtue of an avenging deity, but in virtue of a preventive system of law; not through the presence of a company of fairies, but through that of an admirable organization of police detectives. Of course, the nearer the criminal and the detective are brought home to the reader, the more lively his "sensation." They are brought home to the reader by a happy choice of probable circumstances; and it is through their skill in the choice of these circumstances — their thorough-going realism — that Mr. Collins and Miss Braddon have become famous. In like manner, it is by the thorough-going realism of modern actors that the works of the most poetic of poets have been made to furnish precedent for sensational writers. There are no *circumstances* in "Macbeth", as you read it; but

as you see it played by Mr. Charles Kean or Mr.
Booth it is nothing but circumstances. And we
may here remark, in parentheses, that if the actors
of a past generation — Garrick and Mrs. Siddons
— left with their contemporaries so profound a
conviction of their *greatness*, it is probably because, like the great dramatists they interpreted,
they were ideal and poetic; because their effort
was not to impress but to express.

We have said that although Mr. Collins anticipated Miss Braddon in the work of devising
domestic mysteries adapted to the wants of a
sternly prosaic age, she was yet the founder of
the sensation novel. Mr. Collins's productions
deserve a more respectable name. They are
massive and elaborate constructions — monuments of mosaic work, for the proper mastery of
which it would seem, at first, that an index and
note-book were required. They are not so much
works of art as works of science. To read "The
Woman in White", requires very much the same
intellectual effort as to read Motley or Froude.
We may say, therefore, that Mr. Collins being to
Miss Braddon what Richardson is to Miss Austen,
we date the novel of domestic mystery from the
former lady, for the same reason that we date the
novel of domestic tranquillity from the latter.
Miss Braddon began by a skilful combination of
bigamy, arson, murder, and insanity. These
phenomena are all represented in the deeds of
Lady Audley. The novelty lay in the heroine be-

ing, not a picturesque Italian of the fourteenth century, but an English gentlewoman of the current year, familiar with the use of the railway and the telegraph. The intense probability of the story is constantly reiterated. Modern England — the England of to-day's newspaper — crops up at every step. Of course Lady Audley is a nonentity, without a heart, a soul, a reason. But what we may call the small change for these facts — her eyes, her hair, her mouth, her dresses, her bedroom furniture, her little words and deeds — are so lavishly bestowed that she successfully maintains a kind of half illusion. Lady Audley was diabolically wicked; Aurora Floyd, her successor, was simply foolish, or indiscreet, or indelicate — or anything you please to say of a young lady who runs off with a hostler. But as bigamy had been the cause of Lady Audley's crimes, so it is the cause of Aurora's woes. She marries a second time, on the hypothesis of the death of the hostler. But, to paraphrase a sentence of Thackeray's in a sketch of the projected plot of "Denis Duval", suppose, after all, it should turn out that the hostler was *not* dead? In "Aurora Floyd" the small change is more abundant than ever. Aurora's hair, in particular, alternately blue-black, purple-black, and dead-black, is made to go a great way. Since "Aurora Floyd", Miss Braddon has published half-a-dozen more novels; each, as we have intimated, better than the previous one, and running through more editions;

but each fundamentally a repetition of "Aurora Floyd." These works are censured and ridiculed, but they are extensively read. The author has a hold upon the public. It is, assuredly, worth our while to enquire more particularly how she has obtained it.

The great public, in the first place, is made up of a vast number of little publics, very much as our Union is made up of States, and it is necessary to consider which of these publics is Miss Braddon's. We can best define it with the half of a negative. It is that public which reads nothing but novels, and yet which reads neither George Eliot, George Sand, Thackeray, nor Hawthorne. People who read nothing but novels are very poor critics of human nature. Their foremost desire is for something new. Now, we all know that human nature is very nearly as old as the hills. But *society* is for ever renewing itself. To society, accordingly, and not to life, Miss Braddon turns, and produces, not stories of passion, but stories of action. Society is a vast magazine of crime and suffering, of enormities, mysteries, and miseries of every description, of incidents, in a word. In proportion as an incident is exceptional, it is interesting to persons in search of novelty. Bigamy, murder, and arson are exceptional. Miss Braddon distributes these materials with a generous hand, and attracts the attention of her public. The next step is to hold its attention. There have been plenty of tales of crime which have not made their authors famous, nor put money in their purses. The reason can have been only that they were not well executed. Miss Braddon, accordingly, goes to work like an artist. Let not the curious public take for granted that, from a literary point of view, her works are contemptible. Miss Braddon writes neither fine English nor slovenly English; not she. She writes what we may call very knowing English. If her readers have not read George Eliot and Thackeray and all the great authorities, she assuredly has, and, like every one else, she is the better for it. With a telling subject and a knowing style she proceeds to get up her photograph. These require shrewd observation and wide experience; Miss Braddon has both. Like all women, she has a turn for color; she knows how to paint. She overloads her canvas with detail. It is the peculiar character of these details that constitute her chief force. They betray an intimate acquaintance with that disorderly half of society which becomes every day a greater object of interest to the orderly half. They intimate that, to use an irresistible vulgarism, Miss Braddon "has been there." The novelist who interprets the illegitimate world to the legitimate world, commands from the nature of his position a certain popularity. Miss Braddon deals familiarly with gamblers, and betting-men, and flashy reprobates of every description. She knows much that ladies are not accustomed to know, but that they are apparently very glad to learn. The names of drinks, the technicalities of the faro-table, the lingo of the turf, the talk natural to a crowd of fast men at supper, when there are no ladies present but Miss Braddon, the way one gentleman knocks another down — all these things — the exact local coloring of Bohemia — our sisters and daughters may learn from these works. These things are the incidents of vice; and vice, as is well known, even modern, civilized, elegant, prosaic vice, has its romance. Of this romance Miss Braddon has taken advantage, and the secret of her success is, simply, that she has done her work better than her predecessors. That is, she has done it with a woman's *finesse* and a strict regard to morality. If one of her heroines elopes with a handsome stable-boy, she saves the proprieties by marrying him. This may be indecent if you like, but it is not immoral. If another of her heroines is ever tempted, she resists. With people who are not particular, therefore, as to the moral delicacy of their author, or as to their intellectual strength, Miss Braddon is very naturally a favorite.

XIII

Eugénie de Guérin's Journal

IF Mademoiselle de Guérin, transcribing from the fulness of her affection and her piety her daily record of one of the quietest lives that ever was led by one who had not formally renounced the world, could have foreseen that within a few years after her death, her love, her piety, her character, her daily habits, her household cares, her inmost and freest thoughts, were to be weighed and measured by half the literary critics of Europe and America, she would, doubtless, have found in this fact a miracle more wonderful than any of those to which, in the lives of her favorite saints, she accorded so gracious a belief. The history of a man or woman of genius prolongs itself after death; and one of the most pleasing facts with regard to that of Mlle. de Guérin is that it was her fate to know nothing of her fame. One of the most unselfish of women, she was spared the experience of that publicity which was the inevitable result of her talents. Genius is not a private fact: sooner or later, in the nature of things, it becomes common property. Mlle. de

"The Journal of Eugénie de Guérin." By G. S. Trébutien. London: 1865.

Guérin pays from her present eminence the penalty of her admirable faculties. If there be in
the seclusion, the modesty, the cheerful obscurity
and humility of her life, an essential incongruity
with the broad light of actual criticism, we may
console ourselves with the reflection that, in so
far as it might, fortune has dealt with her in her
own spirit. It has respected her noble uncon-
sciousness. Her life and her fame stand apart.
Between her own enjoyment of the work and the
world's enjoyment of it intervenes that fact of
her death which completes the one and excuses
the other.

Our own excuse for speaking of Mlle. de Guérin
at this somewhat late day lies in the recent issue
of an English translation of her journal. This
translation is apparently as good as it was likely
to be. In the matter of style, it is our opinion
that Mlle. de Guérin loses as much by translation
as her great countrywoman, Mme. de Sévigné;
and as it is for her style especially that we personally value Mlle. de Guérin, we cannot but
think that an English version of her feelings
would fail, in a very important particular, to represent her — her journal being, indeed, nothing
more than a tissue of feelings, woven as simply,
as easily, as closely, as rapidly, with the same in-
terrupted continuity, as a piece of fireside knitting-
work. It is probable, nevertheless, that the book
will prove acceptable from its character of piety;
and for those who are not acquainted with the

original, it may even, through the translator's faithful sympathy, possess a certain literary charm.

Mlle. de Guérin's journal begins in 1834, when she was twenty-nine years of age, and ceases in 1840. It was strictly a series of daily letters addressed to her brother Maurice, and consigned to a number of blank-books, which he read when each was filled. It may be divided into two parts: the first, covering less than five years, extending to the death of Maurice de Guérin; and the second, covering a year and a half, extending from this event to what we may almost call the real death of Mlle. de Guérin herself — that is, the cessation of that practice of daily communion with her brother which had so long absorbed her most lively energies. She actually survived her brother nine years, a period of which she has left us only that beginning of a record formed by those few pages of her journal which she has inscribed to his departed soul. Her admirers will hardly regret the absence of a more extended chronicle of these weary years. Mlle. de Guérin's thoughts had always been half for heaven and half for Maurice. When Maurice died they reverted, by a pious compromise, to heaven alone, and assumed an almost painful monotony.

The chief figure in Mlle. de Guérin's life, accordingly, is not her own, but that of her brother. He, too, has become famous; he, too, had his genius. The sisterly devotion expressed and implied in every line of Mlle. de Guérin's writing needs, indeed, no such fact as this to explain it. She was nothing of a critic; and for the readers of the journal alone, the simple presumption that Maurice de Guérin was a lovable man is sufficient to account for his supremacy in the life of a woman who lived exclusively in her natural affections. For her, then, he was simply the dearest of her brothers; for us, if we had the space, he would be a most interesting object of study. But we can spare him but a few words. He was by several years Eugenie's junior. Sent to school at a distance at an early age, and compelled subsequently to earn his living in Paris by teaching and writing, his life was passed in comparative solitude, and his relations with his family maintained by letters. His first plan had been to enter the church, and with this view he had attached himself to a small community of theological students organized and governed by Lamennais. The dispersion of this community, however, arrested and diverted his ecclesiastical aspirations; and if he never thoroughly abandoned himself to the world as it stands opposed to the church, his habitual seclusion and temperance are marked by a strictly secular tone. After several years of Paris drudgery he contracted a marriage with a young girl of some fortune. He died at the age of twenty-eight. To ourselves, Maurice de Guerin is a more interesting person than his sister. We cannot, indeed, help regarding the collection recently made of his letters and literary remains as a most valuable contribution to our knowledge of the human mind. What he would have accomplished if time had been more generous towards him, it is difficult to say; but as it is, little can be claimed for him on the ground of his positive achievements. To say that he is chiefly interesting as a *phenomenon* seems but a cold way of looking at one who, in all that we know of his character, inspires us with the most tender affection; and yet so it is that we are tempted to speak of Maurice de Guérin. So it is that we are led to look at every man who is deficient in *will*. This was the case with Guérin. His letters, his diary, his verses, are one long record of moral impotency. He was one of the saddest of men. That he had genius, we think his little prose-poem, entitled "The Centaur", conclusively proves; not a splendid, a far-reaching genius, but nevertheless a source of inspiration which was all his own. His sensibility, his perceptions, were of the deepest. He put imagination into everything that he said or wrote. He has left descriptions of nature which have probably never been excelled, because, probably, nature has never been more delicately perceived. And yet we may be sure that for posterity he will live rather in his sister than in himself. For he is essentially an *imperfect* figure; and what the present asks of the past is before all things completeness. A man is only remembered beyond his own generation by his *results;* and the most that Guérin has left us is a heritage of processes.

If he had lived and grown great, we should assuredly be delighted to peruse the record of his moral and religious *tâtonnements*. But as his whole life was but a fragment, his fragmentary efforts lack that character of unity which is essential to whomsoever, in morals or in letters, is destined to become anything of a classic. Maurice de Guérin's only unity is in his sister.

The singular unity of her own genius, indeed, is such as almost to qualify her for this distinction. As her brother was all complexity, she was all simplicity. As he was all doubt, she was all faith. It seems to us that we shall place Mlle. de Guérin on her proper footing, and obviate much possible misconception, if we say that hers was an essentially *finite* nature. We just now mentioned Mme. de Sévigné. The great charm of Mme. de Sévigné's style is her perfect ability to say whatever she pleases. But as she was chiefly an observer of fashionable society, she was not often tempted to utter very composite truths. Now, Mlle. de Guérin, perpetually engaged in the contemplation of the Divine goodness, finds the right word and the right phrase with the same delightful ease as her great predecessor. With her, as with Mme. de Sévigné, style was a natural gift. Many of the causes of this perfection are doubtless identical in both cases. Both Mme. de Sévigné and Mlle. de Guérin were women of taste and of tact, who, under these conditions, wrote from the heart. They wrote freely and familiarly, without any pre-occupation whatever. They were both women of birth, both *ladies* as we say now-a-days. To both of them there clings an air of purely natural distinction, of implicit subordination to the fact of race, a silent sense of responsibility to the past, which goes far to explain the positive character of their style. When we add to this that in both of them the imaginative faculty was singularly limited, we shall have indicated those features which they possessed in common, and shall have helped to confirm our assertion of the finite quality of Mlle. de Guérin's mind. It was not that she was without imagination; on the contrary, she unmistakably possessed it; but she possessed it in very small measure. Religion without imagination is piety; and such is Mlle. de Guérin's religion. Her journal, taken as a whole, seems to us to express a profound contentment. She was, indeed, in a certain sense, impatient of life, but with no stronger impatience than such as the church was able to allay. She had, of course, her moments of discouragement; but, on the whole, she found it easy to believe, and she was too implicit a believer to be unhappy. Her peculiar merit is that, without exaltation, enthusiasm, or ecstacy, quietly, steadily, and naturally, she entertained the idea of the Divine goodness. The truth is that she was strong. She was a woman of character. Thoroughly dependent on the church, she was independent of everything else.

XIV

The Belton Estate

HERE, in the natural order of events, is a new novel by Mr. Trollope. This time it is Miss Clara Amedroz who is agitated by conflicting thoughts. Like most of Mr. Trollope's recent heroines, she is no longer in the first blush of youth; and her story, like most of Mr. Trollope's recent stories, is that of a woman standing irresolute between a better lover and a worse. She first rejects the better for the worse, and then rejects the worse for the better. This latter movement is final, and Captain Aylmer, like Crosbie, in "The Small House at Allington", has to put up with a red-nosed Lady Emily. The reader will surmise that we are not in "The Belton Estate" introduced to very new ground. The book is, nevertheless, to our mind, more readable than many of its predecessors. It is comparatively short, and has the advantage of being a single story, unencumbered by any subordinate or coordinate plot. The interest of Mr. Trollope's main narrative is usually so far from being intense that repeated interruption on behalf of the

"The Belton Estate." By Anthony Trollope. Philadelphia : 1866.

actors charged with the more strictly humorous
business is often very near proving altogether
fatal. To become involved in one of his love
stories is very like sinking into a gentle slumber;
and it is well known that when you are aroused
from your slumber to see something which your
well-meaning intruder considers very entertaining, it is a difficult matter to woo it back again.
In the tale before us we slumber on gently to the
end. There is no heroine but Miss Clara Amedroz,
and no heroes but her two suitors. The lady loves
amiss, but discovers it in time, and invests her
affections more safely. Such, in strictness, is the
substance of the tale; but it is filled out as Mr.
Trollope alone knows how to fill out the primitive
meagreness of his dramatic skeletons. The three
persons whom we have mentioned are each a
character in a way, and their sayings and doings,
their comings and goings, are registered to the
letter and timed to the minute. They write a
number of letters, which are duly transcribed;
they make frequent railway journeys by the
down-train from London; they have cups of tea
in their bedrooms; and they do, in short, in the
novel very much as the reader is doing out of it.
We do not make these remarks in a tone of complaint. Mr. Trollope has been long enough before
the public to have enabled it to take his measure.
We do not open his books with the expectation of
being thrilled, or convinced, or deeply moved in
any way, and, accordingly, when we find one to

be as flat as a Dutch landscape, we remind ourselves that we have wittingly travelled into Hol-
land, and that we have no right to abuse the
scenery for being in character. We reflect, moreover, that there are a vast number of excellent
Dutchmen for whom this low-lying horizon has
infinite charms. If we are passionate and egotis-
tical, we turn our back upon them for a nation of
irreclaimable dullards; but if we are critical and
disinterested, we endeavor to view the prospect
from a Dutch stand-point.

Looking at "The Belton Estate", then, from
Mr. Trollope's own point of view, it is a very
pleasing tale. It contains not a word against
nature. It relates, with great knowledge, humor,
and grace of style, the history of the affections of
a charming young lady. No unlawful devices are
resorted to in order to interest us. People and
things are painted as they stand. Miss Clara
Amedroz is charming only as two-thirds of her
sex are charming — by the sweetness of her face
and figure, the propriety of her manners, and the
amiability of her disposition. Represented thus,
without perversion or exaggeration, she engages
our sympathy as one whom we can understand,
from having known a hundred women exactly
like her. Will Belton, the lover whom she finally
accepts, is still more vividly natural. Even the
critic, who judges the book strictly from a reader's
stand-point, must admit that Mr. Trollope has
drawn few better figures than this, or even (what

is more to the purpose) that, as a representation, he is an approach to ideal excellence. The author understands him well in the life, and the reader understands him well in the book. As soon as he begins to talk we begin to know and to like him, as we know and like such men in the flesh after half an hour of their society. It is true that for many of us half an hour of their society is sufficient, and that here Will Belton is kept before us for days and weeks. No better reason for this is needed than the presumption that the author does not tire of such men so rapidly as we: men healthy, hearty, and shrewd, but men, as we take the liberty of declaring, utterly without mind. Mr. Trollope is simply unable to depict a *mind* in any liberal sense of the word. He tried it in John Grey in "Can You Forgive Her?" but most readers will agree that he failed to express very vividly this gentleman's scholarly intelligence. Will Belton is an enterprising young squire, with a head large enough for a hundred prejudices, but too small for a single opinion, and a heart competent — on the condition, however, as it seems to us, of considerable generous self-contraction on her part — to embrace Miss Amedroz.

The other lover, Captain Aylmer, is not as successful a figure as his rival, but he is yet a very fair likeness of a man who probably abounds in the ranks of that society from which Mr. Trollope recruits his characters, and who occurs, we venture to believe, in that society alone. Not that there are not in all the walks of life weak and passionless men who allow their mothers to bully their affianced wives, and who are utterly incompetent to entertain an idea. But in no other society than that to which Captain Aylmer belongs do such frigidity and such stupidity stand so little in the way of social success. They seem in his case, indeed, to be a passport to it. His prospects depend upon his being respectable, and his being respectable depends, apparently, on his being contemptible. We do not suppose, however, that Mr. Trollope likes him any better than we. In fact, Mr. Trollope never fails to betray his antipathy for mean people and mean actions. And antipathetic to his tastes as is Captain Aylmer's nature, it is the more creditable to him that he has described it so coolly, critically, and temperately. Mr. Trollope is never guilty of an excess in any direction, and the vice of his villain is of so mild a quality that it is powerless to prejudice him against his even milder virtues. These seem to us insufficient to account for Clara's passion, for we are bound to believe that for her it was a passion. As far as the reader sees, Captain Aylmer has done nothing to excite it and everything to quench it, and, indeed, we are quite taken by surprise when, after her aunt's death, she answers his proposal with so emphatic an affirmative. It is a pleasant surprise, however, to find any of Mr. Trollope's people doing a thing contrary to common-sense. Nothing can be better — always from the Dutch point of view — than the management of the reaction in both parties against their engagement; but to base the rupture of a marriage engagement upon an indisposition on the part of the gentleman's mother that the lady shall maintain an acquaintance of long standing with another lady whose past history is discovered to offer a certain little vantage-point for scandal, is, even from the Dutch point of view, an unwarrantable piece of puerility. But the shabbiness of grand society — and especially the secret meannesses, parsimonies, and cruelties of the exemplary British matron — have as great an attraction for Mr. Trollope as they had for Thackeray; and the account of Clara's visit to the home of her intended, the description of the magnificent bullying of Lady Aylmer, and the picture of Miss Aylmer — "as ignorant, weak, and stupid a poor woman as you shall find anywhere in Europe" — make a sketch almost as relentless as the satire of "Vanity Fair" or the "Newcomes." There are several other passages equally clever, notably the chapter in which Belton delivers up Miss Amedroz to her lover's care at the hotel in London; and in which, secure in his expression elsewhere of Belton's superiority to Aylmer, the author feels that he can afford to make him still more delicately natural than he has made him already by contrasting him, *pro tempore*, very disadvantageously with his rival, and causing him to lose his temper and make a fool of himself.

Such praise as this we may freely bestow on the work before us, because, qualified by the important stricture which we have kept in reserve, we feel that it will not seem excessive. Our great objection to "The Belton Estate" is that, as we read it, we seemed to be reading a work written for children; a work prepared for minds unable to think; a work below the apprehension of the average man and woman, or, at the very most, on a level with it, and in no particular above it. "The Belton Estate" is a *stupid* book; and in a much deeper sense than that of being simply dull, for a dull book is always a book that might have been lively. A dull book is a failure. Mr. Trollope's story is stupid and a success. It is essentially, organically, consistently stupid; stupid in direct proportion to its strength. It is without a single idea. It is utterly incompetent to the primary functions of a book, of whatever nature, namely — to suggest thought. In a certain way, indeed, it suggests thought; but this is only on the ruins of its own existence as a book. It acts as the occasion, not as the cause, of thought. It indicates the manner in which a novel should *not*, on any account, be written. That it should deal exclusively with dull, flat, commonplace people was to be expected; and this need not be a fault; but it deals with such people as one of themselves; and this is what Lady Aylmer would call a "damning" fault. Mr. Trollope is a good observer; but he is literally nothing else. He is apparently as incapable of disengaging an idea as of drawing an inference. All his incidents are, if we may so express it, *empirical*. He has seen and heard every act and every speech that appears in his pages. That minds like his should exist, and exist in plenty, is neither to be wondered at nor to be deplored; but that such a mind as his should devote itself to writing novels, and that these novels should be successful, appears to us an extraordinary fact.

XV

Swinburne's "Chastelard"

"CHASTELARD" is not destined, in our judgment, to add to the reputation of the author of "Atalanta in Calydon." It has been said — we know not on what authority — that it is an early production, which the author was encouraged to publish by the success of the latter work. On perusal, this rumor becomes easily credible. "Chastelard" bears many signs of immaturity. The subject, indeed, is one which a man might select at any age; but the treatment of it, as it seems to us, is that of a man still young. The subject is one of the numerous flirtations of Queen Mary of Scotland, which makes, like so many of the rest, a very good theme for a tragedy. A drama involving this remarkable woman has, by the fact of her presence alone, a strong chance of success. The play or the novel is half made by the simple use of her name. Her figure has been repeatedly used, and it is likely it will continue to be used for a long time to come; for it adapts itself to the most diverse modes of treatment. In poetry, after all, the great point is that the objects

---

"Chastelard: A Tragedy." By Algernon Charles Swinburne. New York: 1866.

of our interest should be romantic, and from every possible point of view Queen Mary answers this requisite, whether we accept her as a very conscientious or as a very profligate woman; as a martyr or simply as a criminal. For the fact remains that she was supremely unhappy; and when to this fact we add the consideration that she was in person supremely lovely, that she embodied, if not all the virtues, at least all the charms, of her sex, we shall not be at loss to understand the ready application of her history to purposes of sentiment. And yet, whoever takes her in hand is held to a certain deliberate view of her character — the poet quite as much as the historian. Upon the historian, indeed, a certain conception is imposed by his strict responsibility to facts; but the poet, to whom a great license is usually allowed in the way of modifying facts, is free to take pretty much the view that pleases him best. We repeat, however, that upon some one conception he is bound to take his stand, and to occupy it to the last. Now, the immaturity of Mr. Swinburne's work lies, if we are not mistaken, in his failure to make very clear to himself what he thought about his heroine. That he had thought a great deal about her, we assuredly do not doubt; but he had failed to think to the purpose. He had apparently given up all his imagination to his subject; and, in so doing, had done well; but it seems to us that in this process his subject had the best of the bargain; it gave him very little in return.

Mr. Swinburne has printed at the beginning of his play a short passage from that credulous old voyager, Sir John Mandeville, wherein he speaks of a certain isle toward the north, peopled by beautiful and evil women with eyes of precious stones, which, when they behold any man, forthwith slay him with the beholding. The author's intention, then, has been to indicate a certain poetic analogy between these fatal sirens and his heroine. The idea is pretty; the reader makes the *rapprochement* and proceeds; but when, as he advances in his reading, it dawns upon him that it is upon this idea, as much as upon any other appreciable one, that the tragedy rests, he experiences a feeling of disappointment which, we are bound to say, accompanies him to the end. He recurs to the title-page and finds another epigraph, from Ronsard, which the author has very prettily translated in the body of the play:

"With coming lilies in late April came
  Her body, fashioned whiter for their shame;
  And roses, touched with blood since Adam bled,
  From her fair color filled their lips with red."

The reader's growing disappointment comes from his growing sense of the incompetency of any idea corresponding at all exclusively with these poetic fancies to serve as the leading idea of the work. Out of this disappointment, indeed, there comes a certain quiet satisfaction; the satisfaction, namely, of witnessing the downfall of a structure reared on an unsound basis. Mr.

Swinburne, following the fashion of the day, has endeavored throughout his work to substitute color for design. His failure is, to the reader's mind, an homage to truth. Let us assuredly not proscribe color; but let us first prepare something to receive it. A dramatic work without design is a monstrosity. We may rudely convey our impression of the radical weakness of "Chastelard" by saying that it has no backbone. The prose of the poetry just referred to — that salutary prose which, if we mistake not, intervenes between poetic thought and poetic expression — is that Mary was superlatively fascinating to the sense and superlatively heartless. To say, in poetry, that a woman slays a man with her jewelled eyes, is to mean in prose that she causes every man to love her passionately, and that she deceives every man who does love her. As a woman of this quality, if we fully disengage his idea, Mr. Swinburne accepts Queen Mary — in other words, as a coquette on the heroic scale. But we repeat that this idea, as he handles it, will not carry his play. His understanding of Mary's *moyens* begins and ends with his very lively appreciation of the graces of her body. It is very easy to believe that these were infinite; it was, indeed, in Mr. Swinburne's power to make us know absolutely that they were. It were an impertinence to remind him how Shakespeare makes us know such things. Shakespeare's word carries weight; he speaks with authority. The plot of Mr. Swinburne's play,

if plot it may be called, is the history of the brief
passion aroused by Mary in the breast of the
French adventurer who gives his name to the
work. He has followed her to Scotland and keeps
himself under her eye; she encourages his devotion, but, meanwhile, marries Darnley. On the
night of her marriage he makes his way into her
presence, and she makes him half welcome. Thus
discovered, however, in the *penetralia* of the palace,
he is arrested and cast into prison. Death is the
inevitable result of his presumption. Mary, however, by a bold exercise of her prerogative, pardons
him and sends him an order of release, which,
instead of using, he destroys. Mary then visits
him just before his execution, and, in a scene
which appears to us an equal compound of radical
feebleness and superficial cleverness, finds him
resolved to die. The reader assists at his death
through the time-honored expedient of a spectator
at a window describing the scene without to a
faint-hearted companion within. The play ends
with these pregnant lines:

"Make way there for the lord of Bothwell; room —
Place for my lord of Bothwell next the Queen."

There is, moreover, a slight under-plot, resting
upon the unrequited passion of Mary Beaton, the
queen's woman, for Chastelard, and upon her
suppressed jealousy of her mistress. There is
assuredly in all this the stuff of a truly dramatic
work; but as the case stands, it appears to us that
the dramatic element is flagrantly missed. We

can hardly doubt, indeed, that there was an intention in the faint and indefinite lines in which
all the figures but that of the Queen are drawn.
There is every reason to suppose that Mr. Swinburne had advisedly restricted himself to the
complete and consistent exhibition of her character
alone. Darnley, Murray, and the four Marys are
merely the respective signs of a certain number of
convenient speeches. Chastelard, too, is practically a forfeit, or, rather, he and Mary are but one.
The only way, in our judgment, to force home upon
the reader the requisite sense of Mary's magical
personal influence was to initiate him thoroughly
into its effects upon Chastelard's feelings. This,
we repeat, Mr. Swinburne has not even attempted
to do. Chastelard descants in twenty different
passages of very florid and eloquent verse upon
the intoxicating beauties of his mistress; but
meanwhile the play stands still. Chastelard is
ready to damn himself for Mary's love, and this
fact, dramatically so great, makes shift to reflect
itself in a dozen of those desperately descriptive
speeches in which the poetry of the day delights.
Chastelard is in love, the author may argue, and
a lover is at best a highly imaginative rhapsodist.
Nay, a lover is at the worst a man, and a man
of many feelings. We should be very sorry to be
understood as wishing to suppress such talk as
Chastelard's. On the contrary, we should say —
let him talk as much as he pleases, and let him
deal out poetry by the handful, the more the

better. But meanwhile let not the play languish, let not the story halt. As for Mary, towards whom the reader is to conceive Mr. Swinburne as having assumed serious responsibilities, we may safely say that he has left her untouched. He has consigned her neither to life nor to death. The light of her great name illumines his page, and here and there the imagination of the cultivated reader throbs responsive to an awakened echo of his own previous reading. If Mr. Swinburne has failed to vivify his persons, however, if he has failed to express his subject, he has at least done what the unsuccessful artist so often turns out to have done: he has in a very lively manner expressed *himself*. "Atalanta in Calydon" proved that he was a poet; his present work indicates that his poetic temperament is of a very vigorous order. It indicates, moreover, that it is comparatively easy to write energetic poetry, but that it is very difficult to write a good play.

BY HENRY JAMES

XVI

Kingsley's "Hereward"

MR. KINGSLEY has written nothing better
than this recital of the adventures of Hereward, son of the famous Lady Godiva of Coventry, and the "grim earl", Leofric, her husband —
who as a boy, under King Edward the Confessor,
was outlawed, as too hard a case for his parents
to manage; who took service with foreign princes
and turned sea-rover on his own account; who
was the last of the Berserkers and the first of the
knights-errant; who performed unparalleled feats
of valor and of cunning; who on the Duke of
Normandy's invasion of England felt himself,
in spite of his outlawry, still an Englishman at
heart, sailed over to England, and collected an
army to contest the Norman rights; who contested
them long and bravely, in the fen-country of
Lincolnshire, but at last found the invaders too
many for him and was driven for a subsistence to
the greenwood, where he set the fashion to Robin
Hood and the dozen other ballad-heroes whom
the author enumerates; who under his reverses
grew cold and faithless to the devoted wife whom

"Hereward, the Last of the English." By Charles Kingsley.
Boston : 1866.

139

he had married out of Flanders, and who had
followed his fortunes over land and sea; who,
repudiating Torfrida, thought to patch up his
prospects by a base union with a Norman princess,
for whom he had cherished an earlier but an unworthy passion, and by a tardy submission to the
new king; but who at last, disappointed, humil-
iated, demoralized by idleness, fell a victim, in his
stalwart prime, to the jealousy of the Norman
knights.

Mr. Kingsley's hero, as the reader sees, is an
historical figure, duly celebrated in the contem-
porary and other chronicles, Anglo-Saxon and
Norman. How many of his adventures are fiction does not here signify, inasmuch as they were
destined to become fiction in Mr. Kingsley's novel;
and, as the elements of a novel by a man of genius,
become animated with a more lively respectability
than could ever accrue to them as parcels of du-
bious history. For his leading points, Mr. Kingsley abides by his chroniclers, who, on their side,
abide by tradition. Tradition had made of Hereward's adventures a most picturesque and romantic story; and they have assuredly lost none
of their qualities in Mr. Kingsley's hands. Hereward is a hero quite after his own heart; one
whose virtue, in the antique sense, comes ready-
made to his use; so that he has to supply this
article only in its modern significance. The last
representative of unadulterated English grit, of
what is now the rich marrow of the English char-

acter, could not, with his generous excesses and
his simple shortcomings, but forcibly inspire our
author's imagination. He was a hero, covered
with those glories which as a poet, of an epic
turn, as an admirable story-teller and describer,
and as an Englishman, Mr. Kingsley would delight to relate; and he was a man, subject to those
masculine foibles over which, in his ecclesiastical
and didactic character, our author would love to
moralize. Courage has ever been in Mr. Kingsley's view the divine fact in human nature; and
courage, as bravely understood as he understands
it, is assuredly an excellent thing. He has done
his best to make it worthy of its high position;
his constant effort has been to prove that it is not
an easy virtue. He has several times shown us
that a man may be rich in that courage which is
the condition of successful adventure, but that
he may be very much afraid of his duty. In fact,
almost every one of his heroes has been compelled to make good his heroism by an act of
signal magnanimity. In this manner Kingsley
has insisted upon the worthlessness of the greatest natural strength when unaccompanied by a
corresponding strength of soul. One of his remote
disciples has given a name to this unsanctified
offset the title of the tale, "Barren Honors."
The readers of "Two Years Ago" will remember,
moreover, the pathetic interest which attached
in that charming novel to the essentially unregenerate manfulness of Tom Turnall. The lesson

of his history was that it behooves every man to
devote his muscle — we can find no better name
for Mr. Kingsley's conception of intelligence —
to the service of strict morality. This obligation is the constant theme of Mr. Kingsley's
teaching. It is true that, to his perception, the
possibilities of human character run in a very
narrow channel, and that a man has done his
grandest when he has contrived not to shirk his
plain duty. Duty, for him, is a five-barred gate
in a hunting-field: the cowards dismount and
fumble at the unyielding padlock; the "gentlemen" ride steadily to the leap.

It has been hinted how "Hereward" turns out
a coward. After a long career of generous hack-
ing and hewing, of the most heroic brutalities and
the most knightly courtesies, he finds himself face
to face with one of the homely trials of private
life. He is tired of his wife, who has lost her
youth and her beauty in his service, and he is
tempted by another woman who has been keeping both for him through all the years of his
wanderings. To say, shortly, that he puts away
his wife and marries his unworthy temptress would
be to do him injustice. This is what he comes to,
indeed; but, before judging him, we must learn in
Mr. Kingsley's pages how *naturally* he does so.
Hereward is an instance of that "demoralization"
by defeat of which we have heard so much within
the last five years. He is purely and simply a
fighting man, and with his enormous fighting

capacity he may not unfitly be taken to represent, on a reduced scale, the susceptibilities of a
whole modern army. When, at last, his enemies
outnumber him, he loses heart and, by a very
simple process, becomes good for nothing. This
process — the gradual corrosion in idleness of a
practical mind of the heroic type — is one which
Mr. Kingsley is very well qualified to trace; and
although he has troubled himself throughout very
little with the psychology of his story, and has
told it as much as possible in the simple objective
tone of the old chroniclers to whom he so constantly refers, he has yet, thanks to the moraliz-
ing habit which he is apparently quite unable
entirely to renounce, given us a very pretty insight into poor Hereward's feelings.

It is the absence of the old attempt at philosophy
and at the writing of history which makes the
chief merit of "Hereward" as compared with the
author's other tales. Certain merits Mr. Kingsley
has in splendid fulness, but the metaphysical
faculty is not one of them; and yet in every
one of his writings hitherto there has been a stub-
born philosophical pretension. There is a certain
faculty of story-telling as complete and, used in
no matter what simplicity, as legitimate and hon-
orable as any other; and this gift is Mr. Kingsley's.
But it has been his constant ambition to yoke it
with the procedure of an historian. An important
requisite for an historian is to know how to handle
ideas, an accomplishment which Mr. Kingsley

lacks, as any one may see by turning to his lectures on history, and especially to the inaugural lecture, in which he exhibits his views on the philosophy of history. But in the work before us, as we have said, he has adhered to his chroniclers; and as there is a world of difference between a chronicler and an historian, he has not been tempted to express many opinions. He has told his story with great rapidity and vivacity, and with that happy command of language which makes him one of the few English writers of the present moment from whose style we derive a positive satisfaction. He writes in all seriousness, and yet with a most grateful suppression of that aggressively *earnest* tone which has hitherto formed his chief point of contact with Mr. Carlyle. He writes, in short, as one who enjoys his work; and this fact it is which will give to "Hereward" a durable and inalienable value. The book is not, in our opinion, what historical novels are so apt to become — a *pastiche*. It represents a vast amount of knowledge, of imagination, and of sympathy. We have never been partial to Mr. Kingsley's arrogance, his shallowness, his sanctified prejudices; but we have never doubted that he is a man of genius. "To be a master," as we were told the other day, "is to be a master." "Hereward" is simply a masterpiece, in the literal sense of the term, and as such it is good to read. This fact was supreme in our minds as we read it, and it seemed more forcibly charged than ever before with the assurance of the author's peculiar genius. What is this genius? It lies, in the first place, as it seems to us, in his being a heaven-commissioned *raconteur;* and, in the second place, in his being a consummate Englishman. Some of them are better Englishmen than others. Mr. Kingsley is one of the best. By as much as he is insufferable when he dogmatizes like a schoolboy upon the characteristics of his nation, by so much is he admirable and delightful when he unconsciously expresses them. No American can see these qualities embodied in a work of art without a thrill of sympathy. "Hereward" is an English story — English in its subject, in its spirit, and in its form. He would be a very poor American who, in reading it, should be insensible to the charm of this fact; and he would be a very poor critic who should show himself unable to distinguish between Mr. Kingsley a master and Mr. Kingsley — not a master.

XVII

Winifred Bertram

"WINIFRED BERTRAM" is, in our judgment, much better than the author's preceding work: it is in fact an excellent book of its class. This class it is difficult to define. Were it not that in a certain chapter where Sunday literature is brought into question, the author fails to express her sympathy with it in a manner so signal as almost to suggest an intent to deprecate, we should say that her own book was fashioned on this principle. The chief figure in Miss Winifred Bertram's world, and one quite overshadowing this young lady, is a certain Grace Leigh, who, albeit of a very tender age, is frequently made the mouth-piece of the author's religious convictions and views of life. She is so free from human imperfections, and under all circumstances gravitates so infallibly and gracefully towards the right, that her attitude on any question may almost be taken to settle that question for spirits less clearly illumined. She administers a quiet snub to "Sunday books" by declaring that she possesses none. "I do not think Shakespeare is

"Winifred Bertram and the World She Lived In." [By Mrs. E. R. Charles.] New York: 1866.

quite one," she adds, "nor Homer, although it often helps me on Sundays, and every day, to think of them." The truth is, however, that this young lady is so instinctive a respecter of Sunday that she can very well afford to dispense with literary stimulus. Wherever we place this work, its generous and liberal tone will assure it a respectable station; but is the author confident that she has not been liberal even to laxity in the comprehensive *bienveillance* which she attributes to Miss Grace Leigh, when the latter affirms that "all sermons are nice"? It is true that she qualifies her assertion by the further remark that "at least there is something nice in them", namely, the text. But the whole speech is a very good illustration of the weaker side of the author's spirit. It is indeed the speech of a child, and may have been intended to indicate her character rather than to express a truth of the author's own intelligence. Nevertheless, as we have said, this precocious little maiden is somehow invested with so decided an air of authority, that even when she is off her stilts the reader feels that he is expected to be very attentive. Now the word *nice* as applied to a sermon is thoroughly meaningless; as applied to a Scripture text it is, from the author's point of view, almost irreverent. And yet the reader is annoyed with a suspicion that the author fancies herself to have conveyed in these terms a really ponderable truth. Here is another instance of the same gushing optimism. Having put forward the startling proposition that "everything is pleasant" — it will be observed that our young friend is of a decidedly generalizing turn — Miss Grace Leigh proceeds to confirm it as follows: "It is pleasant to wake up in the morning and think how much one has to do for people — and it is pleasant to mend father's things — and it is pleasant to help the Miss Lovels with their scholars — and it is pleasant to make the cold meat seem like new to father by little changes — and it is pleasant that Mr. Treherne [the landlord] is a greengrocer and not a baker, because there are never any hot, uncomfortable smells — and," to conclude, "it is pleasant that there is a corner of the churchyard in sight." In other words, we would say, with all deference, it is pleasant to be able to be sentimental in cold blood. This pleasure, however, is to the full as difficult to grasp as the converse luxury of being reasonable in a passion.

In spite of this defect, it is very evident that it has been the author's aim to advocate a thoroughly healthy scheme of piety. She had determined to supersede the old-fashioned doctrinal tales on their own ground; to depict a world in which religious zeal should be compatible, in very young persons, with sound limbs and a lively interest in secular pastimes; in which the practice of religious duties should be but the foremost condition of a liberal education. This world of Miss Winifred Bertram is, accordingly, a highly accomplished one. It recalls those fine houses with violet window-panes, in whose drawing-rooms even the humblest visitors are touched with a faint reflection of the purple. Sin and sorrow assume a roseate hue. Candid virtue wears the beautiful blush of modesty. We have seen how the little girl above quoted gets "help" from Homer and Shakespeare. So every one about her is engaged in helping and being helped. She herself is the grand centre of assistance, in virtue, we presume, of her being in direct receipt of this favor from the great sources just mentioned. She walks through these pages shedding light and bounty, counsel and comfort; preaching, prescribing, and chiding. She makes as pretty a figure as you could wish; but she is, to our mind, far too good to be true. As the heroine of a fairy tale she would be admirable, but as a member of this working-day world she is almost ridiculous. She is a nosegay of impossible flowers — of flowers that do not bloom in the low temperature of childhood. We firmly believe that children in pinafores, however rich their natural promise, do not indulge in extemporaneous prayer, in the cogitation of Scripture texts, and in the visitation of the poor and needy, except in very conscious imitation of their elders. The best good they accomplish is effected through a compromise with their essentially immoral love of pleasure. To be disinterested is among the very latest lessons they learn, and we should look with suspicion upon a

little girl whose life was devoted to the service of
an idea. In other words, children grow positively
good only as they grow wise, and they grow wise
only as they grow old and leave childhood behind
them. To make them good before their time is
to make them wise before their time, which is a
very painful consummation. The author justifies
the saintly sagacity of little Grace Leigh by the
fact of her having been obliged to look out for
herself at a very tender age; but this very competency to the various cares and difficulties of her
position, on which the author dwells so lovingly,
is to us a thoroughly unpleasant spectacle. An
habitually pre-occupied child is likely to be an
unhappy one, and an unhappy one — although,
like Mr. Dickens's Little Nell, she may never do
anything naughty — is certainly little more than
an instrument of pathos. We can conceive of
nothing more pernicious for a child than a pre-
mature sense of the seriousness of life, and, above
all, of that whole range of obligations to which
Miss Grace Leigh is so keenly sensitive — the
obligations of charity, the duties of alms-giving.
Nothing would tend more to make a child insuffer-
ably arrogant than the constant presence of a
company of pensioners of its own bounty. Children are essentially democratic, and to represent
the poor as in a state of perpetual dependence on
them is to destroy some of their happiest traits.

But there is a great deal in these pages which
is evidently meant for the parents of the little

boys and girls who read them. There is, for instance, the episode of the conversion of Mrs. O'Brien from elegant carelessness, and heedlessness of her opportunities for beneficence, to an ingenious and systematic practice of philanthropy. We have no doubt that many idle women with plenty of money may derive considerable profit from the perusal of Mrs. O'Brien's story. And there is a great deal more which they may find equally entertaining and instructive — many a forcible reminder of the earnestness of life, and of the fact that by taking a friendly interest in their cooks and housemaids, and bestowing kindly words and thoughts as well as loaves and purses upon the inhabitants of tenement-houses, they may diminish the sum of human misery. We agree with the author that there is a wise way of giving alms as well as a foolish one, and that that promiscuous flinging of bounty which saves the benefactor all the trouble of enquiry and of selection is very detrimental. But, in our opinion, it is especially detrimental to the active party. To the passive one — the pauper — it is of comparatively little importance whether assistance is given him intelligently or not. We should say, indeed, that the more *impersonally* it is given, the better for both parties. The kind of charity advocated with such good sense and good feeling in these pages, is as good as any charity can be which is essentially one with patronage. To show that patronage may be consistent with humility has

been — practically, at least — the author's aim.
In the violet-tinted atmosphere of Miss Winifred
Bertram's world, this may be so, but hardly, we
conceive, in the daylight of nature. Such books
as these — books teaching the rich how to give —
should always carry a companion-piece showing
the poor how to take. The objects of the enlightened charity practised in these pages are
invariably very reasonable as well as very sentimental. A little wilfulness, a little malice, a little
blockheadedness, a little ingratitude, and the position of the alms-dealer becomes very ungraceful;
and Miss Winifred Bertram's companions are
nothing if not graceful. As a serious work, accordingly, we do not deem this account of them
very strong. As an exhibition of a very beautiful
ideal of life by a person who has felt very generously on the subject, it deserves all respect; but
we cannot help feeling that religion and human
nature, and good and evil, and all the other objects of the author's concern, are of very different
aspect and proportions from those into which she
casts them. Nevertheless, her book may be read
with excellent profit by all well-disposed persons:
it is full of incidental merit, and is uncommonly
well written. Little girls, we suppose, will read it
and like it, and for a few days strive to emulate
Grace Leigh. But they will eventually relax their
spiritual sinews, we trust, and be good once more
in a fashion less formidable to their unregenerate
elders.

XVIII

Mrs. Gaskell

WE cannot help thinking that in "Wives and Daughters" the late Mrs. Gaskell has added to the number of those works of fiction — of which we cannot perhaps count more than a score as having been produced in our time — which will outlast the duration of their novelty and continue for years to come to be read and relished for a higher order of merits. Besides being the best of the author's own tales — putting aside "Cranford", that is, which as a work of quite other pretensions ought not to be weighed against it, and which seems to us manifestly destined in its modest way to become a classic — it is also one of the very best novels of its kind. So delicately, so elaborately, so artistically, so truthfully, and heartily is the story wrought out, that the hours given to its perusal seem like hours actually spent, in the flesh as well as the spirit, among the scenes and people described, in the atmosphere of their motives, feelings, traditions, associations. The gentle skill with which the reader is slowly involved in the tissue of the story;

"Wives and Daughters." By Mrs. Gaskell. New York: 1866.

the delicacy of the handwork which has perfected every mesh of the net in which he finds himself ultimately entangled; the lightness of touch which, while he stands all unsuspicious of literary artifice, has stopped every issue into the real world; the admirable, inaudible, invisible exercise of creative power, in short, with which a new and arbitrary world is reared over his heedless head — a world insidiously inclusive of him (such is the *assoupissement* of his critical sense), complete in every particular, from the divine blue of the summer sky to the June-bugs in the roses, from Cynthia Kirkpatrick and her infinite revelations of human nature to old Mrs. Goodenough and her provincial bad grammar — these marvellous results, we say, are such as to compel the reader's very warmest admiration, and to make him feel, in his gratitude for this seeming accession of social and moral knowledge, as if he made but a poor return to the author in testifying, no matter how strongly, to the fact of her genius.

For Mrs. Gaskell's genius was so very composite as a quality, it was so obviously the offspring of her affections, her feelings, her associations, and (considering that, after all, it *was* genius) was so little of an intellectual matter, that it seems almost like slighting these charming facts to talk of them under a collective name, especially when that name is a term so coarsely and disrespectfully synthetic as the word genius has grown to be. But genius is of many kinds, and we are almost tempted to say that that of Mrs. Gaskell strikes us as being little else than a peculiar play of her personal character. In saying this we wish to be understood as valuing not her intellect the less, but her character the more. Were we touching upon her literary character at large, we should say that in her literary career as a whole she displayed, considering her success, a minimum of head. Her career was marked by several little literary indiscretions, which show how much writing was a matter of pure feeling with her. Her "Life of Miss Brontë", for instance, although a very readable and delightful book, is one which a woman of strong head could not possibly have written; for, full as it is of fine qualities, of affection, of generosity, of sympathy, of imagination, it lacks the prime requisites of a good biography. It is written with a signal want of judgment and of critical power; and it has always seemed to us that it tells the reader considerably more about Mrs. Gaskell than about Miss Brontë. In the tale before us this same want of judgment, as we may still call it in the absence of a better name, presuming that the term applies to it only as it stands contrasted with richer gifts, is shown; not in the general management of the story, nor yet in the details, most of which are as good as perfect, but in the way in which, as the tale progresses, the author loses herself in its current very much as we have seen that she causes the reader to do.

The book is very long and of an interest so quiet that not a few of its readers will be sure to vote it dull. In the early portion especially the details are so numerous and so minute that even a very well-disposed reader will be tempted to lay down the book and ask himself of what possible concern to him are the clean frocks and the French lessons of little Molly Gibson. But if he will have patience awhile he will see. As an end these modest domestic facts are indeed valueless; but as a means to what the author would probably have called a "realization" of her central idea, *i. e.*, Molly Gibson, a product, to a certain extent, of clean frocks and French lessons, they hold an eminently respectable place. As he gets on in the story he is thankful for them. They have educated him to a proper degree of interest in the heroine. He feels that he knows her the better and loves her the more for a certain acquaintance with the *minutiæ* of her homely *bourgeois* life. Molly Gibson, however, in spite of the almost fraternal relation which is thus established between herself and the reader — or perhaps, indeed, because of it, for if no man is a hero to his *valet de chambre*, it may be said that no young lady is a heroine to one who, if we may so express our meaning, has known her since she was "*so* high" — Molly Gibson, we repeat, commands a slighter degree of interest than the companion figure of Cynthia Kirkpatrick. Of this figure, in a note affixed to the book in apology for the ab-

sence of the final chapter, which Mrs. Gaskell did
not live to write, the editor of the magazine in
which the story originally appeared speaks in
terms of very high praise; and yet, as it seems to
us, of praise thoroughly well deserved. To describe Cynthia as she stands in Mrs. Gaskell's
pages is impossible. The reader who cares to
know her must trace her attentively out. She
is a girl of whom, in life, any one of her friends, so
challenged, would hesitate to attempt to give a
general account, and yet whose specific sayings
and doings and looks such a friend would probably
delight to talk about. This latter has been Mrs.
Gaskell's course; and if, in a certain sense, it shows
her weakness, it also shows her wisdom. She had
probably known a Cynthia Kirkpatrick, a *résumé*
of whose character she had given up as hopeless;
and she has here accordingly taken a generous
revenge in an analysis as admirably conducted as
any we remember to have read. She contents
herself with a simple record of the innumerable
small facts of the young girl's daily life, and leaves
the reader to draw his conclusions. He draws
them as he proceeds, and yet leaves them always
subject to revision; and he derives from the
author's own marked abdication of the authorita-
tive generalizing tone which, when the other characters are concerned, she has used as a right, a
very delightful sense of the mystery of Cynthia's
nature and of those large proportions which
mystery always suggests. The fact is that genius

is always difficult to formulate, and that Cynthia had a genius for fascination. Her whole character subserved this end. Next after her we think her mother the best drawn character in the book. Less difficult indeed to draw than the daughter, the very nicest art was yet required to keep her from merging, in the reader's sight, into an amusing caricature — a sort of commixture of a very mild solution of Becky Sharp with an equally feeble decoction of Mrs. Nickleby. Touch by touch, under the reader's eye, she builds herself up into her selfish and silly and consummately natural completeness.

Mrs. Gaskell's men are less successful than her women, and her hero in this book, making all allowance for the type of man intended, is hardly interesting enough in juxtaposition with his vivid sweethearts. Still his defects as a masculine being are negative and not positive, which is something to be thankful for, now that lady-novelists are growing completely to eschew the use of simple and honest youths. Osborne Hamley, a much more ambitious figure than Roger, and ambitious as the figure of Cynthia is ambitious, is to our judgment less successful than either of these; and we think the praise given him in the editorial note above-mentioned is excessive. He has a place in the story, and he is delicately and even forcibly conceived, but he is practically little more than a suggestion. Mrs. Gaskell had exhausted her poetry upon Cynthia, and she could spare to

Osborne's very dramatic and even romantic predicaments little more than the close prosaic handling which she had found sufficient for the more vulgar creations. Where this handling accords thoroughly with the spirit of the figures, as in the case of Doctor Gibson and Squire Hamley, the result is admirable. It is good praise of these strongly marked, masculine, middle-aged men to say that they are as forcibly drawn as if a wise masculine hand had drawn them. Perhaps the best scene in the book (as the editor remarks) is the one in which the squire smokes a pipe with one of his sons after his high words with the other. We have intimated that this scene is prosaic; but let not the reader take fright at the word. If an author can be powerful, delicate, humorous, pathetic, dramatic, within the strict limits of homely prose, we see no need of his "dropping into poetry," as Mr. Dickens says. It is Mrs. Gaskell's highest praise to have been all of this, and yet to have written "an everyday story" (as, if we mistake not, the original title of "Wives and Daughters" ran) in an everyday style.

XIX

Marian Rooke

THIS is an average novel and a very bad book — a distinction, as it seems to us, easy to understand. There have been many novels, contemptible or ridiculous in point of dramatic interest, which have obtained a respectful attention through the wisdom of their tone or the elevation of their style. There have been others, skilful and absorbing in the matter of plot, which the reader has nevertheless flung aside half-read, as intolerably foolish, or intolerably vicious in spirit. The plot of "Marian Rooke", although it can hardly be called very skilful on the writer's part or very absorbing on the reader's, is yet decently interesting, as plots go, and may readily suffice to the entertainment of those jolly barbarians of taste who read novels only for what they call the "story." "Marian Rooke" has an abundance — a superabundance — of story, a vast deal of incident, of variety, of sentiment, of passion, of description, of conversation, and of that facetious element which no gentleman's novel should be without. These merits, however, are not by

---

"Marian Rooke, or The Quest for Fortune : a Tale of the Younger World." By Henry D. Sedley. New York : 1865.

themselves of so high an order as to justify us to our conscience in an attempt to impose them upon the public recognition; we should have been content to leave their destinies to fortune. The part of duty in the matter, since duty there is, is to point out the defects of the work.

"Marian Rooke", then, is a tale of the "younger world", or, in other words, of life in the United States. If we are not mistaken, it was published in England either just before, or simultaneously with, its appearance in New York; and if on this point, too, we are not wrong in our facts, it met with a warmer welcome on the other side of the water than it has encountered on this, as, indeed, it had every reason to do, inasmuch as we may convey a certain idea of its spirit in saying that, whereas it was written *for* English circulating libraries, it was written only, if we may so express it, *at* American ones. This air of divided nationality which attended its production is an index of a similar feature in the conception of the book. The reader vacillates between setting the author down as a consummate Yankee and dubbing him as a consummate cockney. At one moment he asserts himself an Englishman who has a perilously small amount of learning about the United States, and at another he seems conclusively to prove himself one of our dear fellow-countrymen, with his honest head slightly turned by a glimpse of the carriage going to one of the Queen of England's drawing-rooms. It remains a constant

source of perplexity that he should be at once so
poor an American and so poor an Englishman.
No Englishman ever entertained for New England the magnificent loathing which burns in Mr.
Sedley's pages. What is New England to him or
he to New England that he should thus rack his
ingenuity in her behalf? So divinely disinterested
an hostility was never inspired by a mere interest
in abstract truth. A tour in the United States in
midwinter, with a fatal succession of bad hotels,
exorbitant hack-drivers, impertinent steamboat
clerks, thankless female fellow-travellers, and terrific railway collisions, might possibly create in a
generous British bosom a certain lusty personal
antipathy to our unmannerly democracy; a vehe-
ment, honest expression of which could not fail
to make a chapter of picturesque and profitable
reading. But it takes an emancipated, a disfran-
chised, an outlawed, or, if you please, a disappointed, American to wish us to believe that he
detests us simply on theory. This impression the
author of "Marian Rooke" would fain convey.
Therefore we say we set him down as one of ourselves. But he betrays, incidentally, as we have
intimated, so — what shall we call it? — so lively
an ignorance of our manners and customs, our
method of action and of speech, that this hypothesis also is not without a certain measure of dis-
proof. He has vouchsafed us no information on
the contested point; and this it is that prevents
conjecture from being impertinent, for it is founded

solely upon the evidence of the story itself, which, as a book once fairly and squarely published, is utterly given over to the public use, and to all such probing, weighing, and analyzing as may help the public to understand it. Further reflection, then, on the mooted point leads us to the conclusion that in order to furnish Mr. Sedley with any local habitation whatever we must consider one of the two conflicting elements of his tale as a purely dramatic characteristic. As the conflict lies between his perfect familiarity with some points of American life and his singular and arbitrary ignorance of others, we must decide that either his knowledge or his ignorance is assumed. And as his ignorance is generally not so much an absence of knowledge and of statement as positive false knowledge and false statement, we embrace the hypothesis that his scathing indifference to the facts of the case is the result of a good deal of painful ingenuity. And this is what we have in mind in calling his book at the outset a bad book. A book which, from an avowedly critical standpoint — even if it were a very flimsy novel — should roundly abuse and reprobate all things American, would command our respect, if it did not command our agreement. But a book projected (intellectually) from the midst of us, as the present one betrays itself to have been, intended to strike us by a rebound from the ignorant sympathy of foreign readers, displaying its knowledge of us by the possession of a large number of facts and by the petty perversion of every fact which it does possess, and leaving an issue for escape from the charge of deliberate misrepresentation (so good a Yankee is the author) by a species of implicit self-reference to a community where a certain ignorance of our habits is not more than natural, — a book in which the author has put himself to so much trouble to do such an ugly piece of work, commands neither our agreement nor our respect.

The hero of the tale is the son of a dissolute English gentleman — time-honored and familiar combination! — who, having immigrated to this country, married an American wife. In this manner originated the fatal "kink" in the young man's nature — the conflict between his literal allegiance to the land of his birth and his spiritual affinity with the proud home of his ancestors. Marian Rooke, a burning Creole beauty, the daughter of a rich Louisiana planter, is similarly at odds with fortune, it having been discovered on her father's death that she is the child of a slave. Hence a beautiful bond of sympathy between the two. We do not propose to relate their adventures. It is enough to say that these are cast successively in California, in Europe, in Boston, in Berkshire County, Massachusetts (where the local color becomes quite appalling), and in the city of New York. The hero and heroine are duly joined in matrimony at the close, and subsequently, we are informed, the hero does "yeoman's service" in the late war, on which side the author (still like a shrewd Yankee) refuses to tell us, so leaving in considerable doubt (since so essential a point is perforce slighted) whether he really fought on either. He serves throughout the book as an instrument for eliciting in their utmost intensity the vulgar manners and sordid morals of the American people. He is, probably in view of this fact, the most deeply pathetic character in the whole extent of fiction. We have no space categorically to refute the ingenious accusations which Mr. Sedley has levied upon our manners and our speech. We must content ourselves with saying that as, if they were true, they would tell a sad tale of our vulgarity, so, since they are false, they tell a sad tale of the vulgarity of Mr. Sedley's imagination. What California was, socially, fifteen years ago, we cannot say; but it was certainly not the headquarters of politeness, and we accordingly leave it to Mr. Sedley's tender mercies. But we are better qualified to judge of New York and Boston. Here is a young lady of fashion, of the former city, welcoming her mother's guests at a *conversazione*: "We are very gay to-night, although promiscuous. Talk has been lively. There are a good many ladies round. Pa and Professor Sukkar are conferring on immorality. Pa is speaking now. Hush!" Here is another young lady, with the best blood in the land in her veins, conferring with her mother as to the probable character of the hero, who has just made his *entrée* into New York society: "Heavens, no! Clinton would have never given letters to a politician; whatever his faults, my brother would never have introduced a politician into the family of the Parapets!" "Unless sinning through ignorance, perhaps," suggests the mother. "Ignorance! surely their odious names are familiar enough. To be sure we don't read the detestable newspapers, their organs, but the men do; and I am confident either papa or Clinton would know if Mr. Gifford had been compromised in politics." Having represented every American in his pages, of no matter what station in life, as using a form of the traditional Sam Slick dialect, in which all the humorous quaintness is omitted and all the extravagant coarseness is retained, the author makes generous amends at last by the elegant language which he puts into the mouths of the Parapets, the family of the young lady just quoted; and by the still more elegant distinction which he claims for them. Into various details of their dreary snobbishness we will not plunge. They constitute, in the author's sight, the one redeeming feature of our deplorable social condition; and he assures us that, incredible as the fact may appear, they yet do actually flourish in aristocratic idleness and seclusion in the midst of our universal barbarism. This, surely, is the most unkindest cut of all. It suggests, moreover, fearful reflections as to what our fate would have been had Mr. Sedley been minded to be complimentary.

XX

A Noble Life

NOBLE lives have always been a sort of specialty with the author of "John Halifax." Few novelists, in this age of sympathy with picturesque turpitude, have given us such flattering accounts of human nature, or have paid such glowing tributes to virtue. "John Halifax" was an attempt to tell the story of a life perfect in every particular; and to relate, moreover, every particular of it. The hero was a sort of Sir Charles Grandison of the democracy, faultless in manner and in morals. There is something almost awful in the thought of a writer undertaking to give a detailed picture of the actions of a perfectly virtuous being. Sir Charles Grandison, with his wig and his sword, his high heels, his bows, his smiles, his Johnsonian compliments, his irreproachable tone, his moderation, his reverence, his piety, his decency in all the relations of life, was possible to the author, and is tolerable to the reader, only as the product of an age in which nature was represented by majestic generalizations. But to create a model gentleman in an

"A Noble Life." By Mrs. D. M. M. Craik. New York: 1866.

age when, to be satisfactory to the general public, art has to specify every individual fact of nature; when, in order to believe what we are desired to believe of such a person, we need to see him photographed at each successive stage of his proceedings, argues either great courage or great temerity on the part of a writer, and certainly involves a system of bold co-operation on the reader's side. We cannot but think that, if Miss Muloch had weighed her task more fairly, she would have shrunk from it in dismay. But neither before nor after his successful incarnation was John Halifax to be weighed or measured. We know of no scales that will hold him, and of no unit of length with which to compare him. He is infinite; he outlasts time; he is enshrined in a million innocent breasts; and before his awful perfection and his eternal durability we respectfully lower our lance. We have, indeed, not the least inclination to laugh at him; nor do we desire to speak with anything but respect of the spirit in which he and his numerous brothers and sisters have been conceived; for we believe it to have been, at bottom, a serious one. That is, Miss Muloch is manifestly a serious lover of human nature, and a passionate admirer of a fine man and a fine woman. Here, surely, is a good solid basis to work upon; and we are certain that on this point Miss Muloch yields to none in the force of her inspiration. But she gives us the impression of having always looked at men and women through a curtain of rose-colored gauze. This impediment to a clear and natural vision is nothing more, we conceive, than her excessive sentimentality. Such a defect may be but the exaggeration of a virtue, but it makes sad work in Miss Muloch's tales. It destroys their most vital property — their appearance of reality; it falsifies every fact and every truth it touches; and, by reaction, it inevitably impugns the writer's sincerity.

The volume before us contains the story of an unfortunate man who, born to wealth and honors, is rendered incompetent, by ill-health and deformity, to the simplest offices of life, but whose soul shines the brighter for this eclipse of his body. Orphaned, dwarfed, crippled, unable to walk, to hold a fork, a book, or a pen, with body enough to suffer acutely, and yet with so little that he can act only through servants upon the objects nearest to him, he contrives, nevertheless, to maintain a noble equanimity, to practise a boundless charity, and to achieve a wide intellectual culture. Such is Miss Muloch's noble life, and this time, at least, we do not contest her epithet. We might cite several examples to illustrate that lively predilection for cripples and invalids by which she has always been distinguished; but we defer to this generous idiosyncracy. It is no more than right that the sickly half of humanity should have its chronicler; and as far as the Earl of Cairnforth is concerned, it were a real loss to the robust half that he should lack his poet. For we cannot help thinking that, admirable as the subject is, the author has done it fair justice, and that she has appreciated its great opportunities. She has handled it delicately and wisely, both as judged by its intrinsic merits and, still more, as judged by her own hitherto revealed abilities. She has told her story simply, directly, and forcibly, with but a moderate tendency to moralize, and quite an artistic perception of the inherent value of her facts. A profound sense of the beauty of the theme impels us to say that of course there are many points in which she might have done better, and to express our regret that, since the story was destined to be written, an essentially stronger pen should not have anticipated the task; since, indeed, the history of a wise man's soul was in question, a wise man, and not a woman something less than wise, should have undertaken to relate it. In such a case certain faulty-sketched episodes would have been more satisfactory. That of Helen Cardross's intimacy with the earl, for instance, would probably have gained largely in dramatic interest by the suggestion of a more delicate sentiment on the earl's part — sensitive, imaginative, manly-souled as he is represented as being — than that of a grateful nursling. Such a feat was doubtless beyond Miss Muloch's powers — as it would indeed have been beyond any woman's; and it was, therefore, the part of prudence not to attempt it. Another weak point is the very undeveloped state of the whole incident of the visit of the earl's insidious kinsman. If this had been drawn out more artistically, it would have given a very interesting picture of the moves and counter-moves about the helpless nobleman's chair, of his simple friends and servants, and his subtle cousin.

Good story-tellers, however, are not so plentiful as that we should throw aside a story because it is told with only partial success. When was more than approximate justice ever done a great subject? In view of this general truth, we gladly commend Miss Muloch as fairly successful. Assuredly, she has her own peculiar merits. If she has not much philosophy nor much style, she has at least feeling and taste. If she does not savor of the classics, neither does she savor of the newspapers. If, in short, she is not George Eliot on the one hand, neither is she Miss Braddon on the other. Where a writer is so transparently a woman as she and the last-named lady betray themselves to be, it matters more than a little what kind of woman she is. In the face of this circumstance, the simplicity, the ignorance, the want of experience, the innocent false guesses and inferences, which, in severely critical moods, are almost ridiculous, resolve themselves into facts charming and even sacred, while the masculine cleverness, the social omniscience, which satisfy the merely intellectual exactions, become an almost revolting spectacle. Miss Muloch is kindly, somewhat dull, pious, and very sentimental — she has both the virtues and defects which are covered by the untranslatable French word *honnête*. Miss Braddon is brilliant, lively, ingenious, and destitute of a ray of sentiment; and we should never dream of calling her *honnête*. And, as matters stand at present, to say that we prefer the sentimental school to the other, is simply to say that we prefer virtue to vice.

XXI

Epictetus

THE present edition of Epictetus, as the title-page affirms, rests upon Mrs. Carter's translation, which was published in a clumsy quarto in 1758. On comparing the two versions, we find that the modifications made by the present editor bear chiefly upon the undue quaintness, directness, and familiarity of Mrs. Carter's style. They were undertaken, he intimates, with the hope of popularizing the great Stoic moralist among modern readers. It is a significant fact, in view of this intention, that the present version has altogether a more *literary* air than Mrs. Carter's own, for which, to judge from the long list of aristocratic subscribers that accompanies it, a somewhat exclusive patronage was anticipated. The difference between the two versions is not very great, but it has seemed to us that the alterations made by Mr. Higginson tend to substitute the language of books for the language of talk. This, however, is but as it should be. The language of talk of the present day is quite as literary as the language of books of a hundred years ago.

"The Works of Epictetus." By Thomas Wentworth Higginson. Boston: 1865.

How far under these new auspices Epictetus is destined to become familiar to modern English readers is a difficult question to decide. In every attempted resuscitation of an old author, one of two things is either expressly or tacitly claimed for him. He is conceived to possess either an historical or an intrinsic interest. He is introduced to us either as a phenomenon, an object worthy of study in connection with a particular phase of civilization, or as a teacher, an object worthy of study in himself, independently of time or place. In one case, in a word, he is offered us as a means; in the other case he is offered us as an end. To become popular he must fulfil the latter condition. The question suggested by this new edition of Epictetus is whether or not he is susceptible of a direct modern application. There are two ways of answering this question. One is to attempt an exposition of his character, and, with the reader's sympathy, to deduce thence our reply. The other is to give our opinion at once, and then to proceed to justify it by an exposition of his character. We select the latter course. We agree with the editor, then, that the teachings of Epictetus possess a permanent value, — that they may properly form at least one department in a modern handbook of morals.

Little is known of our author's life. That he was a Greek by birth; that he lived at Rome in the latter part of the first century; that he was a slave, deformed and poor; and that he publicly

discussed philosophy; — these facts make up all
that we know of his history. But these are assuredly enough. As his philosophy was avowedly
a matter of living and acting, we may be sure —
the sympathetic reader of his Discourses cannot
but be sure — that he exemplified it in his own
life and acts. We need to know little of the history of a man whose theory of conduct was so
explicit, so emphatic, so detailed. There is in his
precepts, possessing them even as we do at second hand, a *personal* accent, a tone of honesty, of
sincerity, of feeling, — an expression, so to speak,
of *temperament*, — which gives them a kind of
autobiographical force. Like his great master,
Socrates, — the object of his constant and almost
religious reference, — we know him only as he
stands reported by a disciple. But he has this
advantage, that his disciple was a man of no particular originality. A thoroughly earnest man,
moreover, a man of strong personal influence and
lively idiosyncrasies, such as Epictetus must have
been, may often be more successfully represented
by another than by himself. In an age when
morals and metaphysics were taught by direct
exhortation, and the teacher's authority de-
pended largely upon the accordance of his habits
with his theories; when genius was reflected as
much in the conduct as in the intellect, and was
in fact measured as much by the one as by the
other; and when the various incidents of a man's
natural disposition — that whole range of quali-

ties which in the present day are held to be quite impertinent to public life — increased or diminished the force of his precepts, — in such an age it is probable that the general figure of a philosopher was in the eyes of his disciples a very vivid and absolute fact, and, provided they were neither Xenophons nor Platos, would be strictly respected in their recollections and reports. This is especially likely to have been the case with Epictetus, from the fact that he was a Stoic. The Stoic philosophy is emphatically a practical one, a rule of life: it applies to the day, the hour, the moment. As represented by Epictetus it is as far removed as possible from metaphysics. There is, therefore, no Stoicism of mere principle. And, lastly, there reigns throughout the parts of Epictetus's Discourses such a close mutual consistency as to fix the impression that his life was thoroughly consistent with the whole.

Stoicism is the most absolute and uncompromising system of morals ever accepted by man. We say system of morals, because it is in effect nothing of a philosophy. It is a stifling of philosophy, a prohibition of inquiry. It declares a man's happiness to be wholly in his own hands, to be identical with the strength of his will, to consist in a certain *parti-pris* of self-control, steadfastly maintained. It teaches the absolute supremacy of virtue, — its superiority to health, riches, honor, and prosperity. Virtue consists in a state of moral satisfaction with those things which reason tells us are in our power, and in a sublime independence of those things which are not in our power. It is not in our power to be rich, to be free, to be sound of body. But it is in our power to be resigned to poverty, slavery, and sickness. It is in our power to live philosophically; *i. e.*, patiently, passively, in conscious accordance with the divine part of our nature. It is easy to understand the efficacy of such a doctrine as this in the age of Nero and Domitian, before Christianity had had time to suggest that virtue is not necessarily a servitude, and that the true condition of happiness is freedom. In that age the only hope of mankind was in the virgin human will. Epictetus never once intimates the existence of an idea of *rights*. On the contrary, his whole theory of those things which are not in our power is inconsistent with such an idea. In his view, the conditions of humanity are permanently fixed. Life is beset on every side with poverty and suffering. Slavery is an accepted fact. Every man is subject, as a matter of course, to certain visitations of cruelty and injustice. These are so inevitable, so much a law of the universe, that we must regulate our lives accordingly. To declaim against them, to resist them, to deny them, is out of the question. Our duty is to accept them in order that we may properly reject them. Our own persons are the field of this operation. Over them we have no power; but over ourselves we have an absolute mastery, that is, over our true

selves; not this contemptible carcass, these perish-
able limbs, this fleeting life, — nothing so simple
as that; and yet, if we would but perceive it, something infinitely more simple, — the self-contained,
unencumbered faculty of reason. Within our
own souls we reign supreme. Cruelty and injustice may invade our bodies; the Stoic quietly
awaits them on the threshold of his reason, arrests
their progress, turns them to naught, and covers
them with confusion. "You may hurt me," he
says, "if you can, that is, if I will. I am only
hurt so far as I heed my injuries; but I will not
heed them. I have better things to think of, —
the providence of God, his wisdom, power, and
beauty, and this god-like principle, my own nature,
from which I derive courage, modesty, and religion. You may hurt me and misuse me, and
much good may it do you. It will indeed gratify
you, inasmuch as for you it is I that you perse-
cute; but for me, who am the proper judge, I
would have you know, it is not I, but this miserable body, to which you are welcome."

The age in which this attitude of mind was a
refuge, a rest, a relief, the fruit of a philosophy,
is an age which we cannot adequately conceive
without a strong intellectual effort. And we must
remember that men would not have assumed
it, if, in spite of its apparent difficulties, it had
not opened the wisest course. *Aux grands maux
les grands remèdes.* When injustice was on the
heroic scale, submission had to be on the heroic

scale too. Such were the consolations of a Ro-
manized world. In a brutal age virtue is brutal
as well as vice; and, indeed, we read the moral depression engendered by the Roman decline more
clearly in these utterances of a reactionary piety
than in any record of the flagrant profligacy of the
time. When this was the last word of honest
Paganism, it was high time that Christianity
should arrive; for if vice called for a reform, virtue called for it equally. Christianity was needed
to correct the Roman spirit, generally, — in its
good as well as in its evil manifestations. It was
needed to teach the respect of weakness. The
Stoicism of Epictetus is in its uncompromising
sternness, its harshness, its one-sidedness, its lack
of imagination, a thoroughly Roman principle.
It rests upon common sense. It adapts itself to
only one stand-point, and betrays no suspicion
of the needs of a character different from that of
its teacher. Common sense, in the character of a
kind of *deus ex machina*, has often undertaken the
solution of complex philosophical problems; but
it has solved them only by cutting the knot.

Stoicism, then, is essentially unphilosophic. It
simplifies human troubles by ignoring half of
them. It is a wilful blindness, a constant begging
of the question. It fosters apathy and paralyzes
the sensibilities. It is through our sensibilities
that we suffer, but it is through them, too, that
we enjoy; and when, by a practical annihilation
of the body, the soul is rendered inaccessible to

pain, it is likewise rendered both inaccessible and incompetent to real pleasure, — to the pleasure of action; for the source of half its impressions, the medium of its constant expression, the condition of human reciprocity, has been destroyed. Stoicism is thus a negation of the possibility of progress. If the world, taken at a given moment, were destined to maintain all its relations unchanged forevermore, then the doctrine in question would be the best theory of life within human attainment. But as to the modern mind, there is always a possible future in which to lodge the fulfilment of impossible ideals; for, besides our principle of Christian faith, there exists for the things of this world a kindred principle of Christian hope, Stoicism seems, at the present day, to imply an utter social immobility. And if the majority of mankind became Stoics, it is certain that social immobility would ensue as the result of so general an assumption of passivity. The grand defect of the system is, that it discourages all responsibility to anything but one's own soul. There is a somewhat apocryphal anecdote of Epictetus having said to his master, Epaphroditus, as the latter was about to put his leg into the torture, "You will break my leg"; and, when in a few moments this result was accomplished, of his having quietly added, "Did not I tell you so?" It would be easy to quote this anecdote as an example of great nobleness of soul. But, on reflection, we see that it reveals, from our modern point of view, an astounding moral degradation. It assuredly does not diminish our respect for Epictetus, any more than the tub of Diogenes diminishes our respect for him; but it sets inflexible limits to our consideration for the spirit by which a noble nature was so enslaved. There is no doubt that, on its own ground, Pagan brutality was best refuted by such means as these. But it is equally certain that such means as these are possible only to spirits tainted by the evils which they deplore. It is against the experience of such evils that they react; but as long as the battle is fought on the old ground, the reactionists only half secure our sympathy. To future ages they have too much in common with their oppressors. It is only when the circle is broken, when the reaction is leavened by a wholly new element, that it seems to us to justify itself. The taint of Epictetus is the taint of slavery.

Mr. Higginson tells us, in his Preface, that these Discourses were the favorite reading of Toussaint l'Ouverture. When we add this fact to the fact that Epictetus was himself a slave, — when we view, in connection, the affinity with these principles of two minds elevated, indeed, by the sentiment of liberty, but in a measure debased by the practice of servitude, — we shall approach a perception of the ignoble side of Stoicism. It has occurred to us that we might realize it in the following fashion. Let us imagine a negro slave, under our former Southern dispensation, keenly conscious of all the indignities of his position, and with an intellect of exceptional power, dogmatically making the best of them, preaching indifference to them, and concluding, in fact, that weariness and blows and plantation fare are rather good things, — we shall so take home to our minds the didactic character of Epictetus.

To the vivacity, the consistency, the intensity of belief, the uncompromising frankness of speech with which this character is maintained, we cannot pay too large a tribute of respect. He must have been a wholesome spectacle in that diseased age, .this free-thinking, plain-speaking old man, a slave and a cripple, sturdily scornful of idleness, luxury, timidity, false philosophy, and all power and pride of place, and sternly reverent of purity, temperance, and piety, — one of the few upright figures in the general decline. Of the universal corruption and laxity of character and will he is keenly, almost pathetically, sensible. "Show me some one person," he exclaims, "formed according to the principles which he professes. Show me one who is sick, and happy; in danger, and happy; dying, and happy; exiled, and happy; disgraced, and happy. Show him to me; for, by Heaven, I long to see a Stoic. . . . Do me this favor. Do not refuse an old man a sight which he has never seen. . . . Let any of you show me a human soul, desiring to be in unity with God; not to accuse either God or man; not to be angry; not to be envious; not to be jealous; in a word, desiring from a man to become a god, and in this poor mortal body aiming to have fellowship with Zeus. Show him to me. But you cannot." No indeed, they could not. And yet very little of the energy of Epictetus goes to merely deploring and lamenting the immorality about him. He is indefatigable in reproving, contradicting, and what we should now-a-days call snubbing, his auditors and interlocutors; in reminding them of their duties, in shaming them out of their foibles and vices. He is a merciless critic of all theorists, logicians, and rhetoricians, — of all who fail to take the very highest ground in regard to the duties of a man, and who teach the conscience to satisfy itself with a form of words. He himself has no need of theories; his five senses teach him all he wants to know. "Have these things no weight?" he asks. "Let a Pyrrhonist or an Academic come and oppose them. For my part, I have neither leisure nor ability to stand up as advocate for common sense. . . . I may not be able to explain how sensation takes place, whether it be diffused universally or reside in a particular part, for I find perplexities in either case; but that you and I are not the same person, I very exactly know." Like most men of a deep moral sense, he is not at all inquisitive; he feels very little curiosity concerning the phenomena of the external world. From beginning to end of his Discourses, there is no hint of a theory of nature, of being, or of the universe. He is ready to take all these things as they come, as the work of the gods, and as adding, in their marvellous beauty and complexity, to the debt we owe the gods. But they are no concern of his. His business is with human nature, with the elevation of human character to the divine ideal. To our perception he is very weak as a logician, although he constantly claims to arrive at truth and wisdom by a severe exercise of the reasoning faculty. His nature is pre-eminently a religious one; and it is when he speaks under the impulse of feeling, and with a certain accent of passion, that he is most worth quoting and remembering. There are moments when he talks very much as a modern Christian would talk. "What else can I do, a lame old man, but sing hymns to God? . . . Since I am a reasonable creature, it is my duty to praise God. This is my business. I do it. Nor will I ever desert this post so long as it is permitted me; and I call upon you to join in the same song." Epictetus praises God because he is a reasonable creature; but what he calls reason, we should, in many cases, call faith. His sense of a Divine presence in human affairs never, indeed, rises to enthusiasm or to ecstasy; but it is, nevertheless, very far removed from the *common* sense on which, in treating of our attitude towards the things of this life, he invariably takes his stand. Religious natures are of no particular time, and of no particular faith. The piety of Epictetus was a religious instinct as pure as the devotion of a

Christian saint; that is, it did for him the most that religion can do for any man, — it enabled him to live hopefully in the midst of a miserable world. It enabled him to do so, indeed, only through the exercise of a force of will of which few Christian saints have probably felt the need; for they have rested their hopes on a definite assurance.

The great value of these Discourses, then, to our perception, is not in their philosophy, — for, in strictness, they have none, — but in the reflection they offer of their author's character. Intellectually he was no genius, — he was, if we may use the expression, very slightly intellectual; he was without curiosity, without science, without imagination, — the element which lends so great a charm to the writings of that other Stoic, Marcus Aurelius. He was simply a moralist; he had a genius for virtue. He was intensely a man among men, an untiring observer, and a good deal of a satirist. It was by the *life* of his style that he acted upon his immediate disciples, and it is by the same virtue, outlasting almost two thousand years and a transformation into our modern speech, that he will act upon the readers of to-day. When moral nobleness finds solid expression, there is no limit to its duration or its influence. Epictetus dealt with crude human nature, which is the same in Christians and Pagans, in men of the nineteenth century and men of the first. In every doctrine there are good and bad possibilities, — there is a good and a bad Stoicism.

But a literal Stoicism our present social conditions render, to say the least, difficult. For the majority of mankind society is tender rather than harsh. We have no longer to hold out our necks to unjust persecutors, to bow our heads to gratuitous insults, to wrap our human nakedness in our simple virtue. This is not an heroic age, and it becomes daily more difficult to be gracefully proud. We, therefore, with less danger than earlier generations may accept and apply Epictetus. Such acceptance, indeed, as he may receive at our hands would hardly answer his desires, and would be but another instance of the unceremonious avidity with which the present fashions the past to its needs. The good a man does the world depends as much on the way the world takes him as on the way he offers himself. Let us take Epictetus as we take all things in these critical days, eclectically. Let us take what suits us, and leave what does not suit us. There is no doubt but we shall find much to our purpose; for we still suffer, and as long as we suffer we must act a part.

"I am acquainted with no book," says Mr. Higginson, "in which the inevitable laws of retribution are more grandly stated, with less of merely childish bribery or threatening." The reader of Epictetus will easily discover what is meant by this, and will decide that, explain it by Stoicism or any other name one may choose, it is for this fact that our author is pre-eminently valuable. That no gain can make up for the loss

of virtue is an old story, but Epictetus makes it
new. What is the punishment, he inquires, of
craven spirits? "To be as they are." "Paris,
they say," to quote from another chapter, "was
undone when the Greeks invaded Troy and laid
it waste, and his family were slain in battle. By
no means; for no one is undone by an action not
his own. . . . His true undoing was when he lost
modesty, faith, honor, virtue. When was Achilles
undone? When Patroclus died? By no means.
But when he gave himself up to rage." And in
another place: "I lost my lamp because the thief
was better at keeping awake than I. But for
that lamp he paid the price of becoming a thief,
for that lamp *he lost his virtue and became like a
wild beast.* This seemed to him a good bargain;
and so let it be!" And in still another: "Is there
not a divine and inevitable law, which exacts the
greatest punishments from those who are guilty
of the greatest offences? For what says this law?
Let him who claims what belongs not to him be
arrogant, be vainglorious, be base, be a slave; let
him grieve, let him envy, let him pity; and, in a
word, let him lament and be miserable." "*That
he is unhappy,*" he says elsewhere, "is an addition
every one must make for himself." This is *good*
Stoicism; and to bear it well in mind is neither
more nor less, for us moderns, than to *apply*
Epictetus.

XXII

Victor Hugo's Last Novel

"RELIGION, society, and nature," says M. Victor Hugo in his preface, "such are the three struggles of man. . . . Man deals with difficulty under the form superstition, under the form prejudice, and under the form element. A triple *ananké* weighs upon us: the *ananké* of dogmas, the *ananké* of laws, the *ananké* of things. In 'Notre Dame de Paris' the author has denounced the first; in 'Les Misérables' he has pointed out the second; in the present work he indicates the third."

Great programmes and intentions, even though they be *à posteriori*, are one of M. Victor Hugo's liveliest characteristics. It will, therefore, not surprise any of his old readers to find him calling what a writer less fond of magnificent generalizations would have been content to describe as "a tale of the sea", a picture of "the *ananké* of things." But M. Victor Hugo is a poet, and he embarks upon the deep in a very different spirit from the late Captain Marryat. He carries with him provisions for a voyage all but interminable;

"Les Travailleurs de la Mer." By Victor Hugo. New York: 1866.

he touches at foreign lands whose existence has never been suspected; and he makes discoveries of almost fabulous importance.

The scene of "Les Travailleurs de la Mer" is laid in M. Hugo's adopted home of Guernsey, or rather in great part in — yes, literally *in* — the circumjacent ocean. The story is a very small one in spite of its enormous distensions and inflations. An inhabitant of the island, the proprietor of a very pretty niece, becomes also proprietor, in the early days of the invention, of a very pretty steamer, with which he establishes communication with the coast of France. He employs as captain one Sieur Clubin, a man long noted on the island for his exquisite probity and virtue. One of his chief recommendations to the esteem of his employer is the fact that in former years, when the latter had admitted to partnership a person of doubtful antecedents, by name Rantaine, he had, out of the fulness of his integrity, divined this gentleman's rascality, and had forewarned his master that some fine day Rantaine would decamp with the cash-box. This catastrophe is, indeed, not slow in happening. Rantaine suddenly departs for regions unknown, taking with him fifty thousand francs more than his share of the capital. These three persons, Lethierry, the proprietor of the steamer, Rantaine, and the captain, Clubin, are all described with a minuteness very disproportionate to any part they play in the story. But when M. Victor Hugo picks up a

supernumerary he is not wont to set him down
until he has bedecked him with more epigrams,
anecdotes, formulas, and similes than would furnish forth a dozen ordinary heroes. Lethierry is
famous for his alacrity in rescuing the victims of
shipwrecks. In heavy weather he paces the shore,
scanning the horizon, and if he descries a craft of
any species or degree in need of assistance, he is
soon seen from afar "upright on the vessel, dripping with rain, mingled with the lightning, with
the face of a lion who should have a mane of sea-
foam." After a day spent in this exercise, he goes
home and knits a pair of stockings. He was a
savage, says the author, but he had his elegances.
The chief of these is that he is very fastidious
about women's hands. The reason that he had
never married was probably that he had never
found a pretty enough pair of hands in his own
station of life. He brings up his niece, Déruchette, to take care, above all things, of her
hands. About this young lady M. Hugo says an
enormous number of extravagant and pretty
things. We all know what to expect, however,
when M. Hugo enters upon the chapter *jeune
fille*. "To have a smile", he says at the close of a
rhapsody on this subject, "which, one knows not
how, lightens the weight of the enormous chain
dragged in common by all the living, is — what
else can I call it but divine? Déruchette had this
smile. We will say more. Déruchette *was* this
smile." Rantaine, the villain, is a most formid-

able creature. He is a mass of incongruities. He has been everywhere and everything. "He was capable of all things, and of worse." "He had passed his life in making eclipses — appearing, disappearing, re-appearing. He was a rascal with a revolving light." "He used to say, '*Je suis pour les mœurs*' — I go in for morals." Sieur Clubin is the reverse of Rantaine. His life is all above-board. He is piety, honesty, decency in-carnate. To suspect him is to make one's self suspected. He is like the ermine; he would die of a stain. As we have said, he sails the little steamer from Guernsey to Saint Malo. One of his idio-syncracies is never to forget a face he has seen. At the latter place, accordingly, he recognizes after a number of years the *ci-devant* humbug, Rantaine. He procures a revolver, surprises him on the cliff, just after (unfortunately, as you might say) he has confirmed his identity by push-ing a coast-guard over into the sea; he faces him, and coolly demands a restitution of the fifty thou-sand francs. Such is his address that the for-midable Rantaine complies like a child, and hands over the little box containing the money. Find-ing a surplus of ten thousand francs, Clubin re-turns them, pockets the balance, and dismisses the criminal. All that Clubin desires is to restore to his impoverished employer his dues. Forth-with, accordingly, he gets up steam, and departs for Guernsey, with his fifty thousand francs se-cured in a belt about his waist. On the Guernsey coast, however, the steamer enters a heavy fog, which soon obscures all progress; and to make matters worse at this critical moment, the pilot is drunk. The captain takes the helm and advances boldly through the fog. But a sudden break in the sky shows the vessel to be close upon a terrible shoal, and before it can be avoided a terrific shock indicates that the steamer has struck. The passengers are huddled into a boat, but the captain, who has conducted himself throughout with admirable presence of mind, announces his intention of remaining with the vessel until it goes down. This ideal of heroism is vainly combated; the boat moves away, and the disinterested Clubin is left alone with the ocean, the wreck, and — do you see the point? — the fifty thousand francs. Doubtless, you do not see it yet; for, in the first place, the Sieur Clubin cannot use the money if he will, and then, as we know, he would not if he could. But here comes a grand *coup de théâtre*, one of M. Hugo's own. What if the virtuous Clubin should, after all, be no better than the iniquitous Rantaine, no better than a life-long hypocrite, the would-be murderer of a shipload of innocents?

The author develops this hypothesis in a wonderful chapter entitled "The Interior of a Soul Illumined." A very dark soul indeed is this of Clubin, needing all the rockets and bonfires of M. Hugo's speech to penetrate its dusky recesses. Left alone on the dreadful ocean, this monstrous being bursts into a wicked laugh. He folds his arms and tastes his solitude. He is free, he is rich, he has succeeded. Now he is going to begin. He has "eliminated the world." "There are caverns in the hypocrite," adds the author; "or rather, the whole hypocrite is a single cavern. When Clubin found himself alone his cavern opened. He ventilated his soul." "He had been", we furthermore read, "the Tantalus of cynicism." He now looks upon his honesty as a serpent looks upon his old skin; and as he does so he laughs a second time. But in these delights he does not forget the practical. His plan is to swim ashore (he is a marvellous swimmer), to remain hidden on the coast until a smuggling vessel picks him up, and then to make his way to America. His exultation, however, is but short-lived. As he looks the fog is rent in twain, and he sees that he has lost his way more effectually than he had intended. The fog has served him but too well. He has not struck the small shoal which he had, as he fancied, steered for, but a much larger one further distant from the shore. Instead of having a mile to swim, he has fifteen. Nevertheless he strips and plunges. As he touches bottom he feels his foot seized. Meanwhile the small boat has been picked up by a sloop, and the passengers have brought the evil tidings into the port of Saint Sampson. The good proprietor of the steamer is overwhelmed with grief for the loss of his precious, his unique, his laboriously wrought machinery. It is suggested, however, that it may still be recovered, that it may be disengaged from the double embrace of the wreck and the rocks, and successfully brought ashore. Whereupon Miss Déruchette steps forth and declares that she will marry the man who shall accomplish this herculean labor. Now this young lady has long been adored in silence by a young *amateur* of the ocean, a strange, brooding, melancholy, ill-reputed fellow, a kind of amphibious Werther, whose only outlet for his passion has been, for a number of years, to serenade his mistress with an instrument which M. Hugo repeatedly denominates a "bug-pipe." He accepts the challenge, and straightway betakes himself, alone and unaided, to the fatal shoal between which the hapless vessel stands wedged. Here begins M. Hugo's version of the struggle of man with the elements, "the *ananké* of things" promised in his preface, and a wonderful version it is.

The whole of the second book is devoted to the labors of this new Hercules in wrenching with his single hands the machinery of the steamer from the angry clutch of nature. Gilliatt (such is the hero's name) encamps upon the summit of a great rock hard by the field of his operations, one of a brace of strong brothers which just hold their chins out of water. Here, under the stars, surrounded by the world of waves, he spends the nights of two long months, during which, through hurricane and cold and fever and hunger, thirst, and despair, he gradually, by a combination of cranks and cross-beams and pulleys which, we doubt not, are as admirably self-consistent as the famous camel which the German philosopher evolved from the depths of his moral consciousness, he finally, we say, disenthralls the machinery from the shattered authority of the wreck. To believe so big a story you must understand what an extraordinary personage was this Gilliatt. M. Hugo has smoothed the way by a full analysis of his nature and habits at the opening of the work; but we protest in all gravity that we utterly fail to comprehend him. Physically, he is of those days when there were giants; morally, he is the product of too much reading of M. de Lamartine, Alfred de Musset, and M. Victor Hugo himself. "*La somme*," says the author, "he was simply a poor man who knew how to read and write." Elsewhere, he is "a great troubled mind and a great wild heart." He has thus a certain affiliation with Mr. Carlyle. Again, while he is defying the tempests and tides for the love of Déruchette, he is "a kind of Job of the ocean. But a Job militant, a Job conqueror, a Job Prometheus." There is a vast deal in this long description of his daily battle with the elements which we should like to quote, had we the space. A great deal we should quote for the reader's amusement; but for a few passages we should expect his admiration. Never, we believe, has mere writing gone so far: that is, never was nature so effectually ousted from its place, in its own nominal interest. We have room only for half-a-dozen sentences relative to Gilliatt's adventure with a certain hideous marine animal, called by M. Hugo the *pieuvre:* an enlarged jelly-fish, with tentacles, and eyes of hideous expression. This obscene creature will become famous through M. Hugo's magnificent hyperbole. "Compared with the *pieuvre*," he says, "the old hydras provoke a smile. Homer and Hesiod could only make the Chimaera. God has made the *pieuvre*. When God wishes, he excels in the execrable."

The author then proceeds with solemn iteration to rehearse all the monsters, fabulous and veritable, which have ever been the terror of man, together with their respective death-dealing attributes. The *pieuvre* has none of all these — none of these vulgar agencies of dread. What, then, is the *pieuvre?* It is a sucker. "It is, in appearance, a mere rag floating under water. When at rest it is dust-colored. But enraged it grows violet. Then it throws itself upon you. Fearful sensation! it is soft." Its tentacular thongs garrote you; its contact paralyzes. "It looks scorbutic, gangrenescent. It is disease arranged into a monstrosity." But we will leave M. Hugo the fine illustrations of his own tongue. "*Une viscosité qui a une volonté, quoi de plus effrayable? De la glue pétrie de haine.*" This irresistible creature devours you in such a way as to elicit from M. Hugo the following remark: "Beyond the terrible, being eaten alive, is the ineffable, being drunk alive." This is followed by some characteristic ratiocinations on physiology. Gilliatt comes near being absorbed into the *pieuvre;* but, for the matter of that, we all go into each other. "*Pourriture, c'est nourriture.* Fearful cleaning of the globe! Carnivorous man is an entomber; and life is made of death. . . . We are sepulchres." In spite of this general law, however, Gilliatt defers his burial by decapitating the *pieuvre.* Shortly afterwards, he discovers, in a very nearly submarine cavern, a human skeleton, girded about with a money belt, inside of which is written *Sieur Clubin.* It was not in vain, therefore, that this unfaithful servant had been detained beneath the waters. Gilliatt appropriates, provisionally, the belt, and ultimately arrives at a successful solution of his problem in mechanics. His interruptions, his perils, his sufferings, his visions, must be read in detail. There is a long description of a storm which grazes the sublime and jostles the ridiculous. Detached from its context, any example of the former would, we fear, fail to justify itself to the reader; and, indeed, the nearest approach to greatness in this whole episode is not to be found in particular passages, but in the very magnificent intention of the whole. As for the ridiculous, we cannot but think that it is amply presented by everything that follows Gilliatt's successful return with the rescued and renovated vessel. While Déruchette's uncle is digesting his surprise, gratitude, and joy, Déruchette herself is engaged in a very sentimental *tête-à-tête* in the garden with a young Anglican divine. An involuntary witness of their emotions, Gilliatt immediately withdraws his claims. More than this, he personally superintends the marriage of the young couple, and sees them on board the vessel which, after the wedding, is to convey them to England. And after this, says the superficial reader, he of course goes home and smokes a pipe. But little has such a reader fathomed the depths of this heroic nature. He betakes himself to a well-known spot on the side of a cliff, where a depression in the rock forms, at low tide, a sort of natural chair. Here he seats himself in time to witness the passage of the vessel bearing away Déruchette and her husband. It almost "grazed the cliff", says M. Hugo. There on the deck, in a bar of sunshine, sit the happy young couple, lost in mutual endearments. The vessel moves away toward the horizon, while the tide rises to Gilliatt's feet. As the vessel travels before his unwinking eye, so gradually the water surges about him. It reaches his knees, his waist, his shoulders, his chin: but he moves not. The little birds call to him warningly, but he heeds them not. He sits open-eyed, gazing at the sloop. His eye, says the author, "resembled nothing that can be seen on this earth. That calm and tragic pupil contained the inexpressible." As the distant sloop disappears from the horizon, the eye is hidden, the head is covered, the ocean reigns alone.

Such is M. Victor Hugo's story. The reader will see that, dramatically, it is emphatically *not* what, from the title, it was likely pre-eminently to be — a study from nature. Nature is nowhere: M. Victor Hugo is everywhere; and his work will add very little to our knowledge of anything but himself. It is, in our opinion, the work of a decline. We have not hesitated to speak of it with levity, because we believe it to have been written exclusively from the head. This fact we deeply regret, for we have an enormous respect for M. Victor Hugo's heart.

XXIII

Felix Holt, the Radical

BETTER, perhaps, than any of George Eliot's novels does "Felix Holt" illustrate her closely wedded talent and foibles. Her plots have always been artificial — clumsily artificial — the conduct of her story slow, and her style diffuse. Her conclusions have been signally weak, as the reader will admit who recalls Hetty's reprieve in "Adam Bede", the inundation of the Floss, and, worse than either, the comfortable reconciliation of Romola and Tessa. The plot of "Felix Holt" is essentially made up, and its development is forced. The style is the same lingering, slow-moving, expanding instrument which we already know. The termination is hasty, inconsiderate, and unsatisfactory — is, in fact, almost an anti-climax. It is a good instance of a certain sagacious tendency to compromise which pervades the author's spirit, and to which her novels owe that disproportion between the meagre effect of the whole and the vigorous character of the different parts, which stamp them as the works of a secondary thinker and an incomplete artist. But if such are the

---

"Felix Holt, the Radical." By George Eliot. New York: 1866.

faults of "Felix Holt" or some of them, we hasten to add that its merits are immense, and that the critic finds it no easy task to disengage himself from the spell of so much power, so much brilliancy, and so much discretion. In what other writer than George Eliot could we forgive so rusty a plot, and such *langueurs* of exposition, such a disparity of outline and detail? or, we may even say, of outline and outline — of general outline and of particular? so much drawing and so little composition? In compensation for these defects we have the broad array of those rich accomplishments to which we owe "Adam Bede" and "Romola." First in order comes the firm and elaborate delineation of individual character, of which Tito in "Romola" is a better example than the present work affords us. Then comes that extensive human sympathy, that easy understanding of character at large, that familiarity with man, from which a novelist draws his real inspiration, from which he borrows all his ideal lines and hues, to which he appeals for a blessing on his fictitious process, and to which he owes it that, firm locked in the tissue of the most rigid prose, he is still more or less of a poet. George Eliot's humanity colors all her other gifts — her humor, her morality, and her exquisite rhetoric. Of all her qualities her humor is apparently most generally relished. Its popularity may, perhaps, be partially accounted for by a natural reaction against the dogma, so long maintained, that a woman has no humor.

Still, there is no doubt that what passes for such among the admirers of Mrs. Poyser and Mrs. Glegg really rests upon a much broader perception of human incongruities than belongs to many a masculine humorist. As for our author's morality, each of our readers has felt its influence for himself. We hardly know how to qualify it. It is not bold, nor passionate, nor aggressive, nor uncompromising — it is constant, genial, and discreet. It is apparently the fruit of a great deal of culture, experience, and resignation. It carries with it that charm and that authority which will always attend the assertions of a mind enriched by researches, when it declares that wisdom and affection are better than science. We speak of the author's intellectual culture of course only as we see it reflected in her style — a style the secret of whose force is in the union of the tenderest and most abundant sympathies with a body of knowledge so ample and so active as to be absolutely free from pedantry.

As a story "Felix Holt" is singularly inartistic. The promise of the title is only half kept. The history of the hero's opinions is made subordinate to so many other considerations, to so many sketches of secondary figures, to so many discursive amplifications of incidental points, to so much that is clear and brilliant and entertaining, but that, compared with this central object, is not serious, that when the reader finds the book drawing to a close without having, as it were, brought

Felix Holt's passions to a head, he feels tempted
to pronounce it a failure and a mistake. As a
novel with a hero there is no doubt that it *is*
a failure. Felix is a fragment. We find him a
Radical and we leave him what? — only "utterly
married"; which is all very well in its place, but
which by itself makes no conclusion. He tells
his mistress at the outset that he was "converted
by six weeks' debauchery." These very dramatic
antecedents demanded somehow a group of con-
sequents equally dramatic. But that quality of
discretion which we have mentioned as belonging
to the author, that tendency to avoid extreme de-
ductions which has in some way muffled the crisis
in each of her novels, and which, reflected in her
style, always mitigates the generosity of her
eloquence — these things appear to have shackled
the freedom of her hand in drawing a figure which
she wished and yet feared to make consistently
heroic. It is not that Felix acts at variance with
his high principles, but that, considering their
importance, he and his principles play so brief a
part and are so often absent from the scene. He
is distinguished for his excellent good sense. He
is uncompromising yet moderate, eager yet patient, earnest yet unimpassioned. He is indeed
a thorough young Englishman, and, in spite of
his sincerity, his integrity, his intelligence, and
his broad shoulders, there is nothing in his figure to
thrill the reader. There is another great novelist
who has often dealt with men and women moved

by exceptional opinions. Whatever these opinions may be, the reader shares them for the time with the writer; he is thrilled by the contact of her passionate earnestness, and he is borne rapidly along upon the floods of feeling which rush through her pages. The Radicalism of "Felix Holt" is strangely remote from the reader; we do not say as Radicalism, which we may have overtopped or undermined, but simply as a feeling entertained. In fact, after the singular eclipse or extinction which it appears to undergo on the occasion of his marriage, the reader feels tempted to rejoice that he, personally, has not worked himself nearer to it. There is, to our perception, but little genuine *passion* in George Eliot's men and women. With the exception of Maggie Tulliver in "The Mill on the Floss", her heroines are all marked by a singular spiritual tenuity. In two of her novels she has introduced seductions; but in both these cases the heroines — Hetty, in "Adam Bede", and Tessa, in "Romola" — are of so light a character as to reduce to a *minimum* the dramatic interest of the episode. We nevertheless think Hetty the best drawn of her young women. Esther Lyon, the heroine of the present tale, has great merits of intention, but the action subsides without having given her a "chance."

It is as a broad picture of Midland country life in England, thirty years ago, that "Felix Holt" is, to our taste, most interesting. On this subject the author writes from a full mind, with a wealth of fancy, of suggestion, of illustration, at the command of no other English writer, bearing you along on the broad and placid rises of her speech, with a kind of retarding persuasiveness which allows her conjured images to sink slowly into your very brain. She has written no pages of this kind of discursive, comprehensive, sympathetic description more powerful or more exquisite than the introductory chapter of the present work. Against the solid and deep-colored passages and touches, she has placed a vast number of rustic figures. We have no space to discriminate them; we can only say that in their aggregate they leave a vivid sense of that multiplicity of eccentricities, and humors, and quaintnesses, and simple *bizarreries*, which appears to belong of right to old English villages. There are particular scenes here — scenes among common people — miners, tinkers, butchers, saddlers, and undertakers — as good as anything that the author has written. Nothing can be better than the scene in which Felix interrupts Johnson's canvass in the tavern, or that of the speech-making at Duffield. In general, we prefer George Eliot's low-life to her high-life. She seems carefully to have studied the one from without, and the other she seems to have glanced at from the midst of it. Mrs. Transome seems to us an unnatural, or rather we should say, a superfluous figure. Her sorrows and trials occupy a space disproportionate to any part that she plays.

205

She is intensely drawn, and yet dramatically she stands idle. She is, nevertheless, made the occasion, like all of her fellow-actors, however shadowy they may be, of a number of deep and brilliant touches. The character of her son, the well-born, cold-blooded, and moneyed Liberal, who divides the heroship with Felix, is delicately and firmly conceived; but like the great Tito even, like Mr. Lyon, the Dissenting preacher in the present work, like Esther Lyon herself, he is too long-drawn, too placid; he lacks dramatic compactness and rapidity. Tito is presented to us with some degree of completeness, only because Romola is very long, and because, for his sake, the reader is very patient.

A great deal of high praise has been given to "Felix Holt", and a great deal more will be given still; a great many strong words will be used about the author. But we think it of considerable importance that these should at least go no further than they have already gone. It is no new phenomenon for an English novelist to exhibit mental resources which may avail him in other walks of literature; to have powers of thought at all commensurate with his powers of imagination, that when a writer unites these conditions he is likely to receive excessive homage. There is in George Eliot's writings a tone of sagacity, of easy penetration, which leads us to believe that she would be the last to form a false estimate of her works, together with a serious respect for truth which convinces us that she would lament the publication of such an estimate. In our opinion, then, neither "Felix Holt", nor "Adam Bede", nor "Romola", is a master-piece. They have none of the inspiration, the heat, nor the essential simplicity of such a work. They belong to a kind of writing in which the English tongue has the good fortune to abound — that clever, voluble, bright-colored novel of manners which began with the present century under the auspices of Miss Edgeworth and Miss Austen. George Eliot is stronger in degree than either of these writers, but she is not different in kind. She brings to her task a richer mind, but she uses it in very much the same way. With a certain masculine comprehensiveness which they lack, she is eventually a feminine — a delightfully feminine — writer. She has the microscopic observation, not a myriad of whose keen notations are worth a single one of those great sympathetic guesses with which a real master attacks the truth, and which, by their occasional occurrence in the stories of Mr. Charles Reade (the much abused "Griffith Gaunt" included), make him, to our mind, the most readable of living English novelists, and prove him a distant kinsman of Shakespeare. George Eliot has the exquisitely good taste on a small scale, the absence of taste on a large (the vulgar plot of "Felix Holt" exemplifies this deficiency), the unbroken current of feeling and, we may add, of expression, which distinguishes the feminine mind. That she should be offered a higher place than she has earned, is easily explained by the charm which such gifts as hers in such abundance are sure to exercise.

BY HENRY JAMES

XXIV

The Letters of Eugénie de Guérin

NOW that the friends and correspondents of
Mademoiselle de Guérin have consented to
the publication of her letters, there remains no
obstacle to a thorough acquaintance not only with
the facts of her external life, but with her thoughts
and feelings — the life of her soul. It can have
been the fortune of few persons to become so
widely and intimately known as the author of
these letters, and to have evoked sentiments of
such unalloyed admiration and tenderness. How
small is the proportion either of men or of women
who could afford to have the last veil of privacy
removed from their daily lives; not for an exceptional moment, a season of violent inspiration or
of spasmodic effort, but constantly, uninterrupt-
edly, for a period of seventeen years. Mlle. de
Guérin's letters confirm in every particular the
consummately pleasing impression left by her
journal. A delicate mind, an affectionate heart,
a pious soul — the gift of feeling and of expression
in equal measure — and this not from the poverty
of the former faculty, but from the absolute richness of the latter. The aggregation of these facts

"Lettres d'Eugénie de Guérin." New York: 1896.

again resolves itself under the reader's eyes into a figure of a sweetness so perfect, so uniform, and so simple that it seems to belong rather to the biography of a mediæval saint than to the complex mechanism of our actual life. And, indeed, what was Mlle. de Guérin, after all, but a mediæval saint? No other definition so nearly covers the union of her abundant gentleness and her perfect simplicity. There are saints of various kinds — passionate saints and saints of pure piety. Mlle. de Guérin was one of the latter, and we cannot but think that she needed but a wider field of action to have effectually recommended herself to the formal gratitude of the Church. This collection of her letters seems to us to have every quality requisite to place it beside those *livres édifiants* of which she was so fond — unction, intensity, and orthodoxy.

We have called Mlle. de Guérin a saint perhaps as much from a sense of satisfaction in being able to apply a temporary definition to out predicate as from the desire to qualify our subject. What is a saint? the reader may ask. A saint, we hasten to reply, is — Mlle. de Guérin; read her letters and you will discover. If you are disappointed, the reason will lie not in this admirable woman, but in the saintly idea. Such as this idea is, she answers it — and we have called her, moreover, a mediæval saint. It is true that the organization of society during these latter years has not been favorable to a direct and extensive action on the part of personal sanctity, and that, as we associate the idea of a successful exercise of this distinction with social conditions which have long ceased to exist, it seems almost illogical to imply that saintship is possible among our contemporaries. Yet it is equally certain that men and women of extraordinary purity of character constantly attain to a familiarity with divine things as deep and undisturbed as Mlle. de Guérin's. Her peculiar distinction — that fact through which she evokes the image of an earlier stage of the world's history — is the singular simplicity of her genius and of her circumstances. Nowhere are exquisite moral rectitude and the spirit of devotion more frequent than in New England; but in New England, to a certain extent, virtue and piety seem to be nourished by vice and skepticism. A very good man or a very good woman in New England is an extremely complex being. They are as innocent as you please, but they are anything but ignorant. They travel; they hold political opinions; they are accomplished Abolitionists; they read magazines and newspapers, and write for them; they read novels and police reports; they subscribe to lyceum lectures and to great libraries; in a word, they are enlightened. The result of this freedom of enquiry is that they become profoundly self-conscious. They obtain a notion of the relation of their virtues to a thousand objects of which Mlle. de Guérin had no conception, and, owing to their relations with these objects, they present a myriad of reflected lights and shadows. For Mlle. de Guérin there existed but two objects — the church and the world, of neither of which did it ever occur to her to attempt an analysis. One was all good, the other all evil — although here, perhaps, her rich natural charity arrested in some degree her aversion. Such being her attitude toward external things, Mlle. de Guérin was certainly not enlightened. But she was better than this — she was light itself. Her life — or perhaps we should rather say her faith — is like a small, still taper before a shrine, flickering in no fitful air-current, and steadily burning to its socket.

To busy New Englanders the manners and household habits exhibited in these letters are stamped with all the quaintness of remote antiquity. But for a couple of short sojourns in Paris and in the Nivernais, a journey to Toulouse, and a visit to the Pyrenees shortly before her death, Mlle. de Guérin's life was passed in an isolated château in the heart of an ancient province, without visitors, without books, without diversions; with no society but that of her only sister, a brother, the senior of Maurice, and her father, whom the reader's fancy, kindled by an occasional allusion, depicts as one of the scattered outstanding gentlemen of the old *régime* — proud, incorruptible, austere, devout, and affectionate, and, with his small resources, a keen wine-grower. It is no wonder that, in the social vacuity of her life, Mlle. de Guérin turned so earnestly to letter-writing. Her only other occupations were to think about her brother Maurice, to spin by the kitchen fireside, to read the life of a saint, or at best a stray volume of Scott or Lamartine, or Bernardin de Saint-Pierre; to observe zealously the fasts and festivals and sacraments of the church, and to visit sick peasants. Her greatest social pleasure seems to have been an occasional talk with an ecclesiastic; for to her perception all priests were wise and benignant, and never commonplace. "To-morrow", she writes, "I shall talk sermon. We are to hear the Abbé Roques. He is always my favorite preacher. *It is n't that the others are not excellent.*" There is something very pathetic in the intellectual penury with which Mlle. de Guérin had to struggle, although there is no doubt that the unsuspecting simplicity of vision which charms us in her writing is largely owing to the narrow extent of her reading. The household stock of books was small; it was difficult, both on account of the exiguity of the means of the family and its remoteness from a large town, to procure new ones; and in the case of Mlle. de Guérin herself, the number of available works was further limited by her constant scruples as to their morality. It must be owned that she knew few works of the first excellence. She read St. Augustine and Fénelon and Pascal, but for the most part she got her thoughts very far from the source. Some one gives her Montaigne, but, although she is no longer a young girl, she discreetly declines to open him. "I am reading for a second time," she writes, "Bernardin de Saint-Pierre, an amiable and simple author, whom it is good to read in the country. After this I should like 'Notre Dame de Paris'; but I am afraid. These novels make such havoc that I dread their passage; it terrifies me simply to see their effect on certain hearts. Mine, now so calm, would like to remain as it is." So, instead of the great men, she contents herself with the small. "You see," she elsewhere says, "we are keeping the Month of Mary. I have bought for this purpose at Albi a little book, 'The New Month of Mary', by the Abbé Le Gaillan; a little book of which I am very fond — soft and sweet, like May itself, and full of flowers of devotion. Whoever should take it well to heart would be agreeable to God and *en admiration aux anges.* . . . Read it; it is something celestial."

It is difficult to give an idea of the intimacy, the immediacy, of Mlle. de Guérin's relations with the practice of piety. Not an incident but is a motive, a pretext, an occasion, for religious action or reflection of some kind. She looks at the world from over the top of her *prie-dieu*, with her finger in her prayer-book. "Mlle. d'H.", she writes, "comes to edify me every second day; she reaches church early, confesses herself, and takes the communion with an *air d'ange* that ravishes and desolates me. *How I envy her her soul!* . . . Her

brothers, too, are little saints. The eldest, etc.
. . . Is n't it very edifying?" And again: "I am
in every way surrounded with edification, fed
upon sermons and discourses. Such a good Lent
as I have passed!" Describing to a dear friend,
a young lady of her own age, a peculiar ceremony
which she had witnessed on a young girl's taking
conventual vows: "They say", she concludes,
"that everything the novice asks of God at this
moment is granted her. One asked to die; she
died. Do you know what I would ask? *That you
should be a saint.*" The reader will, of course, be
prepared to find Mlle. de Guérin a very consistent
Catholic — a perfect, an absolute one. This fact
explains her, and we may even say excuses her.
So complete a spiritual submission, so complete
an intellectual self-stultification, would be revolting if they were a matter of choice. It is because
they are a matter of authority and necessity,
things born to and implicitly accepted, that the
reader is able to put away his sense of their funda-
mental repulsiveness sufficiently to allow him to
appreciate their incidental charms. It is the utter
consistency of Mlle. de Guérin's faith, the unin-
terruptedness of her spiritual subjection, that
make them beautiful. A question, a doubt, an
act of will, the least shadow of a claim to *choice*
— these things would instantly break the charm,
deprive the letters of their invaluable distinction,
and transform them from a delightful book into a
merely readable one. That distinction lies in the

fact that they form a work of pure, unmitigated *feeling*. The penalty paid by Mlle. de Guérin and those persons who are educated in the same principles, for their spiritual and mental security, is that they are incapable of entertaining or producing ideas. There is not, to our belief, a single idea, a single thought, in the whole of these pages. On the other hand, one grand, supreme idea being tacitly understood and accepted throughout — the idea, namely, of the Church — and a particular direction being thus given to emotion, there is an incalculable host of feelings. Judge how matters are simplified. Genius and pure feeling! No wonder Mlle. de Guérin writes well! There are, doubtless, persons who would be ill-natured enough to call her a bigot; but never would the term have been so ill applied. Is a pure skeptic a bigot? Mlle. de Guérin was the converse of this, a pure believer. A pure skeptic doubts all he knows; Mlle. de Guérin believes all she knows. She knows only the Catholic Church. A bigot refuses; she did nothing all her life but accept.

The two great events of Mlle. de Guérin's life were her visit to Paris on the occasion of the marriage of her brother Maurice, and his death, in Languedoc, eight months afterwards. Paris she took very quietly, as she took everything. What pleased her most was the abundance and splendor of the churches, in which she spent a large portion of her time. She had changed her sky, but she did not change her mind. The profoundest impression, however, that she was destined to receive was that caused by her brother's death. He died on the best of terms with the Church, from which he had suffered a temporary alienation. Her letters on the occasion of this event have an accent of intense emotion which nothing else could arouse. We cannot do better than translate a portion of one, which seems to us to possess a most painful beauty:

"For a week now since he has left us — since he is in heaven and I am on earth — I have n't been able to speak to you of him, to be with you, to unite with you, my tender friend, also so dearly loved. Shall we never be disabused of our affections? Neither sorrows, nor rupture, nor death — nothing changes us. We love, still love — love into the very tomb, love ashes, cling to the body which has borne a soul; but the soul, we know that is in heaven. Oh, yes! there above, where I see thee, my dear Maurice; where thou art awaiting me and saying, 'Eugénie, come hither to God, where one is happy.' My dear friend, all happiness on earth is at an end; I told you so; I have buried the life of my heart; I have lost the charm of my existence. I did not know all that I found in my brother, nor what happiness I had placed in him. Prospects, hopes, my old life beside his, and then a soul that understood me. He and I were two eyes in the same head. Now we 're apart. God has come between us. His will be done! God stood on Calvary for the love of us;

let us stand at the foot of the cross for the love of him. This one seems heavy and covered with thorns, but so was that of Jesus. Let him help me to carry mine. We shall at last get to the top, and from Calvary to heaven the road is n't long. Life is short, and indeed what should we do on earth with eternity? My God! so long as we are holy, that we profit by the grace that comes from trials, from tears, from tribulations and anguish, treasures of the Christian! Oh, my friend! you have only to look at these things, this world, with the eye of faith, and all changes. Happy Father Trubert, who sees this so eminently! How I should like to have a little of his soul, so full of faith, so radiant with love! . . . How things change! Let us change, too, my friend; let us disabuse ourselves of the world, of its creatures, of everything. I only ask for complete indifference."

BY HENRY JAMES

XXV

The Last French Novel

M. ALEXANDRE DUMAS, the younger, having established a reputation as one of the
most ingenious of playwrights, and the most un-
flinching in his adherence to certain morbid social
types, has now, at one stroke, affixed his name to
the list of the greater French novelists. He had,
indeed, written a number of clever stories; but
in none of them was there discernible a claim
to arrest the public attention. In the "Affaire
Clémenceau" this claim is apparent from the first
page to the last; or, in other words, the work bears
signal marks of being, before all things, *serious*.
It is for this reason that we feel justified in speaking of it.

The story is cast into the shape of a memorial,
drawn up for the use of his advocate by a man
under indictment for the murder of his wife. It
proposes to relate the history of their connection
and to trace out, step by step, every link in a long
chain of provocation. It aims, in fact, at putting
the lawyer — or, in other words, the reader — as
nearly as possible in the position of the accused.

"Affaire Clémenceau: Mémoire de l'Accusé." By Alexandre Dumas. Paris: 1866.

219

It is not a piece of special pleading; it is a patient, intelligent statement of facts. It is not, indeed, a mere dry *catalogue raisonné* of incidents governed only by the spirit of chronology; for the hero is, on the face of the matter, a man of the deepest feeling and the richest understanding. Although the narrative confines itself to facts, these are dealt with in a fashion which of late days it has been agreed to call physiological. Metaphysics have been for some time turning to physiology; novels are following their example. The author concerns himself with motives and with causes, but his process is the reverse of transcendental. He bores his way so keenly and so successfully into the real, that one is tempted to fear that he will come out on the other side, as the French Revolution is said to have done with regard to liberty. In speaking of his book, it behooves the critic honestly to take note of the direction towards which he sets his face. It is evident from the outset that he will deal with things as they are; that he will speak without intellectual prudery and without bravado; that, having to tell a story containing elements the most painful and the most repulsive, he will pursue the one course which may justify his choice: that of exhibiting these elements in their integrity. To adopt such a course, so considerately, so consciously, and yet with so little of that aggressive dogmatism which would be sure to betray the mixed intention of an inferior writer; to pursue it so steadily, so relentlessly, and with so sincere and manful an intelligence of the interests at stake; to do this is, in our opinion, to have accomplished a great work, and to have come very near being a great writer.

Pierre Clémenceau is the natural son of an industrious and successful *lingère*. His misfortunes begin with his going to school, where the circumstances of his birth make him an object of general obloquy. The sufferings of childhood have formed the stock of the first volume of many an English novel, but we do not remember to have read any account of a school-boy's tribulations so natural in outline and so severely sober in color as the bald recital of young Clémenceau's persecution. It has been said, and doubtless with justice, in criticisms of this part of the book, that M. Dumas has fallen quite beside the mark in localizing such a system of moral reprobation in a Parisian school. Let us American readers, then, take it home to ourselves; we shall not have translated the book for nothing. On leaving school, Clémenceau evinces a lively inclination for modelling in clay; some of his figures are shown to a famous sculptor, who gives him hearty encouragement, and kindly consents to receive him as a pupil. From this moment his worldly fortunes prosper. His vocation is plain, he works hard, his talent obtains due recognition. He is still a very young man, however, when he meets at a fancy-dress party, given by a literary lady of the Bohemian order, a singular couple, whose destinies are forthwith interwoven with his own: a showy, middle-aged woman, dressed as Marie de Médicis, and her little daughter, radiant with velvet and childish loveliness, as her page. The child, worn out with late hours, falls asleep in an arm-chair; while she sleeps, Clémenceau, with an artist's impulse, attempts to sketch her figure, and, while he sketches, loses his heart. The child awakes, asks to see the picture, and then asks to possess it. Clémenceau promises to add a few touches at his leisure, and to bring it to her the next morning. This whole scene has been aptly cited as an instance of the author's resolute devotion to the actual and the natural. Nothing could be less ideal, less pastoral, than the dawning of the hero's passion. No privacy, no solitude, no fresh air, no glimpse of nature; but, instead, a shabby-genteel masquerade on a rainy night, the odors of the *pot-au-feu*, an infant phenomenon, and a mamma in hired finery. The acquaintance thus begun soon becomes an intimacy. Madame Dobronowska is a Polish lady who has had misfortunes, and who is leading a hand-to-mouth existence in Paris, in anticipation of the brilliant future to which she regards her daughter's beauty as the key. There follows an elaborate picture of the household of these two ladies, of their mingled poverty and vanity, of the childish innocence and incipient coquetry of the daughter, of the magnificent visions and the plausible garrulity of the mother. Madame Dobronowska is an adventuress

more false and mercenary than the fancy can
readily conceive, but gifted for the ruin of her
victims with a certain strong perfume of frankness,
motherliness, and *bonhomie*, which is the more
fatal because it is partly natural. There is something equally pathetic and hideous in her jealous
adoration of her child's beauty and her merely
prudential vigilance. "Have you seen her hands?"
she asks of Clémenceau, when he comes with his
sketch. "Yes." "Look at them by daylight."
"She raised her daughter's hand and showed me
its truly remarkable transparency by flattening it,
so to speak, against the light; and then, taking it
between her own, she kissed it with a sort of
frenzy, crying, '*Tu es belle ça!*' These words produced upon the child the effect of a cordial; the
color came to her cheeks, she smiled, she had got
back her strength." Clémenceau executes a bust
of the young girl, and makes himself useful to the
mother. Before many weeks, however, his friends
leave Paris to seek their fortunes in Russia. For
three years Clémenceau sees nothing more of
them, although he occasionally receives a letter
from Iza (the daughter) describing the vicissi-
tudes of their career. Failing in her attempt to
secure for her daughter the notice of the Crown
Prince at St. Petersburg, Madame Dobronowska
removes to Warsaw, and commences operations
afresh. As time elapses, however, these operations
prove to be of a nature detrimental to her daughter's honor; and Iza, horrified by her mother's

machinations, which she is now of an age to comprehend, applies for assistance to Clémenceau, as her only friend. The young man replies by a declaration of love, which Iza receives with rapture, and forthwith makes her escape to Paris. She is now seventeen years old, and in the perfection of beauty; Clémenceau's mother is admitted into the secret, and they are married. For a long time their married life is without a cloud; but at last Iza becomes a mother, Madame Dobronowska arrives, a reconciliation takes place, Clémenceau's own mother wastes away from an inexplicable malady, and a number of his friends show signs of leaving him. Finally comes upon him like a thunder-clap the revelation of a long course of exorbitant infidelity on the part of his wife. The woman who has been for him the purest of mortals has long been, for all the world beside, a prodigy of impudicity. Clémenceau breaks with her on the spot, and takes the edge from his frenzy by fighting a duel with the last of her many lovers. He provides for the maintenance of his child, and suffers himself to be led to Rome by one of his friends. Here, in the study of the great monuments of art, he awaits the closing of the wound which has been inflicted upon his honor and upon the deepest passions of his soul. His better wishes, however, are not answered; day by day the desire for revenge, the fury of resentment, gathers instead of losing force. Hearing at last that, after a short term of seclusion, his wife has appeared before the world in a blaze of splendor, as the presumed mistress of a foreign potentate, he hastily returns to Paris and presents himself at the mansion occupied by Iza at the cost of her royal protector. She receives him with the cynical good nature of a soul utterly bereft of shame, and he stabs her to the heart.

Such is a rapid outline of M. Dumas's story. It traces the process of the fatal domination acquired by a base and ignoble soul over a lofty and generous one. No criticism can give an idea of the mingled delicacy and strength of the method by which we are made to witness the unfolding of the heroine's vicious instincts. There is in one of Balzac's novels a certain Valérie Marneffe, who may be qualified as the poetry of Thackeray's Becky Sharpe. Iza Dobronowska is the poetry of Valérie Marneffe. The principle of her being is an absolute delight in her own corporeal loveliness; this principle, taking active force, leads her into the excesses which arrest her career.

We are content to sum up the defects of the "Affaire Clémenceau" in the statement that its ultimate effect is to depress the reader's mind, to leave it with no better compensation for the patient endurance of so many horrors than a grave conviction of the writer's prodigious talent, and a certain vague, irritating suspicion that his own depression is even deeper than ours. In the way of compensation this is not enough. To be completely great, a work of art must lift up the reader's heart; and it is the artist's secret to reconcile this condition with images of the barest and sternest reality. Life is dispiriting, art is inspiring; and a story-teller who aims at anything more than a fleeting success has no right to tell an ugly story unless he knows its beautiful counterpart. The impression that he should aim to produce on the reader's mind with his work must have much in common with the impression originally produced on his own mind by his subject. If the effect of an efficient knowledge of his subject had been to fill his spirit with melancholy, and to paralyze his better feelings, it would be impossible that his work should be written. Its existence depends on the artist's reaction against the subject; and if the subject is morally hideous, of course this reaction will be in favor of moral beauty. The fault of M. Dumas's book, in our judgment, is not that such a reaction has not occurred in his own mind, or even that it has been slight, but that it is but faintly reflected in the constitution of the story. There is in the author's tone an unpleasant suggestion of cynicism. It may be, however, that there is but just enough to show us how seriously, how solemnly even, he has taken the miseries which he describes. There is enough, at any rate, to establish an essential difference between the "Affaire Clémenceau" and such a book as M. Edmond About's "Madelon." It may be, taking high ground, a fault that the former work is depressing; but is it not a greater fault that the latter, considering what it is, is amusing? The work before us thrills and interests the reader from beginning to end. It is hard to give it more liberal praise than to say that, in spite of all its crudities, all its audacities, his finer feelings are never for an instant in abeyance, and although, to our nervous Anglo-Saxon apprehensions, they may occasionally seem to be threatened, their interests are never actually superseded by those of his grosser ones. Since the taste of the age is for realism, all thanks for such realism as this. It fortifies and enlarges the mind; it disciplines the fancy. Since radicalism in literature is the order of the day, let us welcome a radicalism so intelligent and so logical. In a season of careless and flippant writing, and of universal literary laxity, there are few sensations more wholesome than to read a work so long considered and so severely executed as the present. From beginning to end there is not a word which is accidental, not a sentence which leaves the author's pen without his perfect assent and sympathy. He has driven in his stake at the end as well as at the beginning. Such writing is reading for men.